MW01380387

BRING THEM TO ME

Tracy L. Moss

Published by
In Time Publishing & Media Group
75 East Wacker Drive, 10th Floor
Chicago, Illinois 60601
www.intimepublishing.com

ISBN# 0-9715797-3-3

Dedication

Then said I, behold, I come; in the volume of the Book it is written of me; I delight to do your will, O my God; yes, your law is within my heart.

Psalms 40:7

I dedicate this Spirit-led project to the new love in my life. He has shown me that there is hope to a life that seemed as if it had none. He has shown me unconditional love, accepting me just the way I was. He is at this moment restoring my soul and filling it with love. He has replaced my heart with His. He has revealed His desires to me, which were my deepest desires already. He has shown me that obedience comes naturally as I witness His agape love for me no matter what. He has shown me Heaven on earth. He continues to walk with me in the right path while leading me to all that God has for me.

I give an encore to His presence in my life. His name is Jesus, the living God. He is the way, the truth, and the life. May His will be done.

To my precious mother, Geraldine, who I love so much and am proud of every passing day as she also keeps her eyes on Jesus. She has been a great example in my life, and I thank God for choosing her as my mom.

To my brother, for his love and words of wisdom as God would speak through him on many occassions during this process. I am proud of him and his new way of thinking. I thank God for choosing him as my brother.

Dedication continued...

To my loving Grandma Moss; to my best friend and big sister in Christ, Sharon; to the little sister I always wanted, Tracee; to a dear friend, Natasha; and to a new friend in love with Jesus, Ninia.

Special thanks to my publishers and new friends in Christ, Azania and Leonardo, their belief in the words God spoke to me has uplifted and edified me since the first day I walked into their office. Thanks also goes out to their staff. I love you all!

Here's to the ministering angels Tony Stewart and Joseph Hamilton used by God to take me to my next spiritual level.

Special dedication to my Pastor and Teacher - Bill Winston. His faith and obedience has been a great example in my going forward and being all God is calling me to be.

Special dedication to James and Cherrie Upshaw for your faith and support in the vision God has put in me that is manifesting right now, before our eyes.

More importantly, to all whom God has chosen to read this series. All those whose hearts are open to His newness of life. Souls that are hungry for the better they have always imagined and dreamed of. This book will "bring you to Him," in Jesus' name.

Introduction
"Keeping It Real"

Just three days ago on November 12th, I celebrated my 33rd birthday. Not only am I tucking away one more year of experiences both good and bad, I have a story to share with you; a story that up until now I didn't have the courage to reveal.

It took me 32 years to understand, the real reason for my life, my past actions, and more importantly my relationship with God. You have to understand I thought I knew God. I went to church, but throughout that entire time I was keeping God in a box.

I'm going to let you in on who I was; what I've done in my life, and the truth I have finally come to believe and accept. This introduction reveals my life B.C., before I invited Jesus "all the way" into my life. I'm sharing my journal, my daily thoughts both right and wrong in order to help you understand the real me, the "far-from-perfect," "struggling-through-life," and sometimes "too-tired-to-believe" me.

It's all here in these very private letters to the Lord. By "keeping it real," throughout my journal, you will be a witness to my old and new ways of thinking about life. You may even be able to relate and recognize yourself in many of the situations and actions I'm about to share with you. Walk with me during shameful, sinful, and troubling times, as well as when God revealed Himself to me or rather, the times when I let Him in and how my life changed.

God guided me to peace, to a personal relationship with the Lord Jesus Christ and ultimately back to who I am in His eyes—His great expression no matter how my past has defined me. Understand, I never thought I'd be sharing my journal in this way. I agonized about how much to reveal; what would people think about me; is it better to leave the past in the shadows or open up and let the reader in? It was a hard choice, but the Lord reminded me that it's not about me any more, it's about how many lives can be touched and changed. It's about the souls who don't know the Lord and the lost souls who don't know the Lord's purpose for their lives. It's about the lost souls who do not know God in a personal intimate way.

As I began opening myself to the Lord, He showed me more of His light, more of His truth, ultimately bringing me closer to my essence and to Him made available through His Word, the Bible. This was only one of many gifts made available to me as the Lord began ministering to me during this season of prayer in my life. Believe me, you will see why I was empty, why I could not be completely satisfied, and why I was so thirsty for a change that only Jesus could bring. I tried almost everything to fill the void inside of me, everything but Jesus.

Why did I start journaling at this time and not before? I needed help, and I was ready to admit it to God. I opened my heart, released my fear and stood humbly in front of Him. God knew my heart sincerely desired change. Change not just for the moment, for a lifetime. I no longer wanted my results; I wanted God's results. I was tired of being tired!

Tired of being religious (thinking my good works and good intentions would keep me saved). Tired of hearing the Word of God, but not living the Word of God. Tired of not being a woman of word. Tired of feeling loved one day and hated the next. Tired of thinking I was complete and still feeling empty. Tired of hearing "You're the perfect package, but..." Tired of having money and not managing it right. Tired of caring what people thought, (although I said I didn't). Tired if being called a hypocrite. Tired of having friends because of who I knew. Tired of long hours with companics that didn't appreciate it. Tired of no peace. Tired of knowing deep inside there was something better, but never asking God what. Tired of knowing I was wasting precious time.

Precious time was being wasted as I tried to look successful for the world. I was living a fantasy, walking around with a blind-fold on trying to be satisfied with what I could see, touch, and taste. There was always an invisible void that I continuously felt, yet, I kept choosing what was in front of me. I needed help to get on the right path. Life had become an addiction of highs and lows. I was seeking fulfillment from the outside while all along it was my inside, my soul in need of a rehab—**a Jesus rehab**.

For you to understand the path I was on I have to reveal the darkness I came from, the same darkness many of you are unconsciously living in; this same darkness inevitably lead me to diligently seek peace and change in my life. The type of changes in my life I had always dreamed and anticipated, leaving me seeking and searching fulfillment and satisfaction that I could never seem to find completely. As you read, you will find the struggles and confusion I went through on my path to being delivered from childhood curses. When I write or speak on them I find these inner bruises are not as tender as I come into a greater peace with and in my life. My soul was being restored, and made aware of the newness of Christ in me.

In the Bible, individual's weaknesses were not camouflaged; they were God's chosen ones to carry out and share His truth; therefore my weaknesses shall be unveiled. These weaknesses are present examples of what to do and what not to do while you search to break free from a guilty conscious; a same train of thinking that keeps you feeling worthy in God's eyes thus unworthy to step towards Him. Choices that kept me living a plan satan had devised for my life; inevitably keeping me from the perfect plan God had already predestined for me, since the beginning.

I must admit that I was a great sinner for 32 years! I was in bondage to my thoughts. Therefore, doing the same things and getting the same results. I became the great actress that I always professionally pursued to be, but not on the silver screen, as you may think. I had a feature role in a movie called "Death," and the producer was "satan." The dream I was in, and a lot of people still are, was a set-up to give me a breakdown, not a breakthrough. My choices kept me a member of the deceived cast, with a season ticket to pain, loss and failure.

I guess God knew that millions of people could relate to my situation and desire to know Him as I eventually have. So here it is, part one of my journey towards reclaiming who I am and who the Lord has always meant for me to be. God also brought it to my attention that for readers to embrace the purpose of the "Bring Them To Me" journal series and what He is sharing through me, I first need to expand on the world of darkness I was experiencing. My journal begins with me writing notes from a positive prospective (affirmations) to the Lord as I get to know Him by spending time in His Word. I focus on being positive because it was necessary to begin renewing my mind, but you need to know who I was before being Born-again, baptized in

Jesus' Name, and filled with the power of the Holy Ghost.

Offering so much deceit, the world can shake you where you are most vulnerable, where your hearts are most dear—your family. At one point, the main catalyst to my seeking a better life was my family's salvation. As I watched my mother assume the role of both parents, (doing whatever it took to make sure we were taken care of) I actually thought I could save us; but I went about it the "world's way." I was too intelligent to let God in; to do it God's way—the Divine way. As the years eroded away, the world began to take its toll. My single mother raised my brother and me under a blanket of unexplainable and unconditional love. (Just like God has for all His children.) I never had a father, when I was seven months in my mother's womb and my brother was at the age of eighteen months our dad was accidentally shot by his best friend while breaking up a fight. "Love equals us three," is our favorite saying; there was nothing we could do to shake her love even when lack, drug use, rehabs and prison began to devour my family's resolve.

In my latter years, I also fell under some of these same attacks, though I strived to keep them hidden from my family and the world. I needed a way for us to be set free from generational curses (things the world says you should be because your parents, grandparents, and so forth were), but I did not know how to go about breaking these shackles. I'm sorry but lack, drug use, sickness and prison are not inherited from relatives; it is inherited by your own thinking. Indeed, my thoughts were holding me captive in the physical world when my freedom existed in the Spirit. The type of freedom I could experience here on earth not just in Heaven.

I was living a life God had not intended for me, just like so many of us today. Bottom line is, I was a "world pleaser" and not a "God pleaser." Tracy L. Moss, had two personalities. One was caught in a world of lies, darkness, and deceit. The other was a young girl at heart who loved cartoons and carried a visible innocence and knowing that there was better for me. I know God did not make me the way I was, the world did along with my choices.

I tried so hard to give love, but true love did not dwell in me because I was spiritually dead, ("Men where the most destructive..."). Lust was the common denominator for most of my relationships. I dated men that saw me as their god. Satan knew exactly how I was thinking because he was the father of my thoughts. He is not creative.

And when the devil had ended every (the complete cycle of) temptation, he (temporarily) left Him (that is, stood off from Him) until another more opportune and favorable time.

Luke 4:13 AMP

Satan presents the same obstacles and distractions over and over. It was up to me to stop choosing his creations—men who had big hearts but whom also lead secret lives. Being a man/world pleaser I did whatever it took to show I cared; to stay pleasing in the eyes of the world. Sometimes that meant losing my integrity when all I wanted in return was love and approval from outside of myself. I was seeking something only my absent spirit could fill. There was always an invisible void that I continuously felt deep inside and as I kept choosing what was in front of me I was going on a down escalator that was taking me deeper into darkness.

I needed a relationship with Jesus in order to find true peace. No man or worldly thing could restore my soul, like the intimacy of getting to know God. Only the Spirit of the living God could come in and restore me to be all that He was calling me to be. My good intentions could not do it, my money could not do it, my relationships could not do it. My family could not do it; only the Spirit of God could show me newness in this life. The Lord told me to not be ashamed of the "old Tracy," she is no longer. Once I was Born-again, baptized in Jesus' Name and filled with the gifts of the Holy Spirit, the world met a "new Tracy." I became the "real" Tracy with the Spirit of God residing in me. I was refreshed with a true inner peace and the restoration of my heart and soul has begun. I have been resurrected just like Jesus. I have forgiven my past because the Spirit of God has given me the grace to do so. The past was a time of war not with what I could see physically but with what I could not see spiritually. The dark, the path many of us unconsciously follow because we do not let God into our daily life. I had to stop letting religion tell me it was my works and good intent that pleased God; it was by Jesus' works on the cross from which God's grace saved and placed me in good-standing with Him.

It is my hope, for all to open their hearts and accept the reality that God is real and so is His son, Jesus. God has a plan and so does satan. Jesus, the way, the truth, and the life is God's plan. Death is satan's. Jesus was God's revelation and Divine plan to save a decaying world, not just then but also right now! You must know my friend, there is a life prepared for us when we depart this world, for those who love God and live according to His purpose. The question is, "How many are called, but never come?"

I know you have an ear to hear and a heart that is open because you have come to these words. God is speaking. God is teaching. God is moving. This is just one of His many ways to share His goodness with us that we might use our free will to choose to learn His ways. Walk with me as I go from gory to glory in part one of this two-part journal series. Learn from the lesson's God has shared with me from the beginning of my deeper walk with Him and how He has moved me swiftly into my true calling. It was not an overnight process for me, nor will it be for you. Realize just as I have, that you will need to give God as much time to restore your soul as was given to corrupt it. Obedience is the key! Being obedient is not only honoring the Ten Commandments, it is saying no to your flesh (worldly ways) and yes to your Spirit (His ways) because God's perfect plan for you is presented to your Spirit not to your flesh.

Come into the Lord's presence with me, His ways and the Holy Spirit's true purpose here on earth. The Lord reminds me that I can never stop learning from Him; witness as I am delivered from my past, guided from darkness and back into God's presence. My process is three-fold. Follow me as I am delivered from **Sin** (world pleaser); to **Self** (self pleaser); to a **Spirit**-led life (God pleaser). Let me bring you to Him in this first journal.

"Now, go, write it before them on a tablet and inscribe it in a book, that it may be as a witness for the time to come forevermore."

Isaiah 30:8 AMP

Letter To My Daughter:

My precious daughter,

"Just a closer walk with Thee, precious Jesus is my plea ..."

What a beautiful work of Art! God is truly with you! This is the most inspiring reading of my life! I couldn't expect better! This journal of truths, awareness in Christ, and geniality (gives credibility to "keeping it real"). It is truly spirit-led!
Thank you for sharing it with me and giving me an opportunity to read it before you published it! I feel elated!

I never really accepted the responsibility of "obedience" to God before reading your journal. I've always been a carefree person who relied on my paternal parents. They always came through for me in times of need. I breath a genuine sigh of relief in knowing that God, loves us more than we could ever deserve and that there is someone like you standing in the gap for someone like myself. My parents, as you know are no longer with me ... it sure feels good to know that God's always there, just waiting for us to turn our lives over to Him and let His Will be done.

You have always been a shinning star ... bringing light into the life of those who were struggling. I knew that God had blessed you upon your birth. He adopted you and took the place of your dead father. He instilled in you the love of Christ ... He will be with you always and will walk with you through all of your life's experiences. I believe you will receive your prayer requests, answered in full, within the year 2004.

Keep your faith and love for God always. Continue to focus on God's love and love for self, and others. You will be able to receive the quality kindness and devotion you deserve and your hard work and efforts will not go unrewarded.

I'm sure your brother will be proud of your book. I can hardly wait for him to read it and comment.

One last word, you strive to please ... God has chosen you for your desire to please, but he will use this rare quality to direct pleasure your way, in and through Christ, pleasing you double fold! So, continue to sow your seeds of faith. Keeping God first and foremost in your life. We both know the end results!

May God Bless and keep you always. In the mighty name of Jesus, amen!

Love you ... It is us three, plus (+)

Your mother,
Geraldine Gage-Moss

Need I tell you how very, very proud of you I am. Surely, God will continue to shape, mold, and perfect you and give to you your heart's desire. You, deserve it!

SIN

What shall we say (to all this)? Are we to remain in sin in order that God's grace (favor and mercy) may multiply and overflow? Certainly not! How can we who died to sin live in it any longer? Are you ignorant of the fact that all of us who have been baptized in Christ Jesus were baptized into His death?

Let not sin therefore rule as king in your mortal (short-lived perishable) bodies, to make you yield to its cravings and be subject to its lusts and evil passions.

Romans 6:1-3, 12 AMP

✍ **MAN/WORLD PLEASER:** lives by man's wisdom (philosophical viewpoints about God); becoming aware of God intellectually; Lack of spiritual knowledge; no relationship with God; Body and soul (Spirit comes and goes because of walk in flesh); backslider; residence at the altar repenting (not sincerely desiring change); spoon fed God's Word (scripture by scripture by my pastor and not myself): Believer with little faith; never feeling completely satisfied/void apparent in my life; dependent on all five senses (see, touch, taste, feel and smell); Fear of the unknown; Emotional; Lack self-control; Ignorance to satan, because focus is on the positive only; Titled "So Spiritual" by the world (caressing the ego); guilty conscious; good intentions thinking that this will save; no inner peace; **yet another Spiritual level to go.**

November 15, 2001   Thursday   5:56 p.m.

Dear God,

This afternoon was very peaceful. I found a quiet spot in a park where I was able to read the Bible. Took care of some business via cell phone and napped on my blanket. Thank you for this spot God, I tend to come here a lot to have some "me" time without any distractions. I'm surrounded with your creations (trees, flowers, animals) none of which can disturb me. Also, I have a sore throat that seems to be getting better.

Earlier I was with my boyfriend Mark, at his house, but felt the need to go home. It's mainly because he was only focused on how he's going to make his dollars for the remainder of the year. No time to be concerned with my sickness or presence. So I left. I believe it's good to be focused, but you should also have a balanced life, not just all work or all play. With him it's one or the other, no compromise.

Spiritually, I feel focused, and that's where my strength is coming from to help me deal with the lack of communication in our relationship. I'm learning *not to force anything, to let You, God work in my life. I don't ever want to feel like I'm settling for something or someone who doesn't treat me the way that I deserve to be treated. But I'm also learning how to not be so picky, realizing that people and opportunities come into your life for a reason. It may not be for a lifetime, I just take it day by day.*

I love You and thank You God daily for all things big and small!

He has made everything beautiful in its time. He also has planted eternity in men's heart and minds (a divinely implanted sense of a purpose working through the ages which nothing under the sun but God alone can satisfy), yet so that men cannot find out what God has done from the beginning to the end.

Ecclesiastes 3:11 AMP

❧ The world tells us that if you "settle" things are bound to get better. THAT'S A LIE! There is no need to "settle" in a relationship when you know within that you deserve better! God has placed this deep knowing in your heart since the beginning. A better relationship comes when you first seek a relationship with God; then man.

December 9, 2001   Sunday   Evening

Dear God,

I pray for a decision about whether to go to Arizona for peace and prayer time. My ex-boyfriend Eddie is currently vacationing there and has invited me down to hang out with him during his off-season. We have been "just friends" now for some time ever since our mutual breakup occurred a few years ago. I've shared with him the struggles of my current relationship with Mark, and how it's up and down. I told him I just needed some time to get away and clear my head, to focus more on my spiritual growth. Should I go God?

I need to know if I will fall into his "muscular" arms and his "sweet-talk" (like before). Does he really want to help, or will he try to sweep me off my feet and into bed. Will I lose myself on this get away?

But those who wait for the Lord (who expect, look for, and hope in Him) shall change and renew their strength and power; they shall lift their wings and mount up (close to God) as eagles (mount up to the sun); they shall run and not be weary, they shall walk and not faint or become tired.

Isaiah 40:31 AMP

🌿 Getting away will not erase the challenges you face daily. Once you return, the problem is still present. Stop running, the battle is not yours. It's the Lord's. Turn the problem over to the Lord and rest in the knowing that He will bring an answer and/or resolution.

December 18, 2001   Tuesday   p.m.

Dear God,

Thank you for hearing my requests and sharing in my decision-making. I need you.

I had a deep knowing that "no" was the answer to my going to Arizona, so I didn't go. It obviously was not a good time at that moment, but I did decide to go to his hometown a week later where he invited me to see a restaurant named after him, to share in some of his new accomplishments. He mentioned my having plenty of quiet time during my stay, plenty of me time.

During this stay I reflected on how my choices have molded my life. How my choices will continue to shape my life for the better or worse. I meditated and I prayed. I realized that I must know God in order to choose "better," to live "better."

Although temptation did not present itself, I discovered an old pattern of running from one male friend to the other for comfort. I know I need to learn how to be by myself. I always seemed to have a "spare" friend, just in case.

🌿 Satan can send you curses wrapped like a blessing. It is your responsibility to learn when to look deeper than just the packaging or situation to discover patterns in your life that lead you away from God.

I desire change in every area God, as I seek the truth about who I really am.

For let him who wants to enjoy life and see good days (good-whether apparent or not) keep his tongue free from evil and his lips from guile (treachery, deceit). Let him turn from wickedness and shun it, and let him do right. Let him search for peace (harmony; undisturbedness from fears, agitating passions, and moral conflicts) and seek it eagerly. (Do not merely desire peaceful relations with God, with your fellow-men, and with yourself, but pursue, go after them!)

1 Peter 3:10-11 AMP

❧ Instead of running to the phone, you should run to the throne of God for His guidance and direction in your life. Being alone with God will not be a lonely time, rather a time of love, strength, and insight. Learn to be still in God's presence wherever you are.

December 28, 2001   Friday   6 a.m.

Fasting with Prayer 6 a.m.-6 p.m.

Dear God,

As I pray to You for Your goodness, for Your guidance, for Your strength, for Your direction, and for Your will, I shall fast and restrain from giving my body what it desires the most, food. I must say no to myself today and learn to give up something I can't seem to do without. This will take me slowly toward gaining self-control. I will eventually have control of my body, instead of it having control over me. I know this will not be an overnight process, but I must continue to indulge in fasting on a regular basis.

❧ We live of the flesh, of the ego. The first step towards God inevitably begins with rejecting what the body desires, money, fame, sex, drinking, etc. You need to learn to control the body, because up until now your body has controlled your life, a life of suffering, anger, confusion, and loss.

I know that by myself I can do nothing; it is "You" who strengthens me!

Desires I pray for and questions I need answers to:

I pray for my continued knowledge of faith and having it at all times ... "I do believe in the unseen." Faith.

I pray for a prosperous career opportunity that will offer longevity, profitability, stability, and respect.

I pray for a renewed relationship with my family. "Detachment with love attached." My eagerness to change or to control the outcome of situations in their life has only caused them to be comfortable in what they are doing. They refuse to accept responsibility of wrong decisions as long as they have me to lean-on. I realize that the best support I can give them is to first, pray for them, and second, to let go and let God. This is love – tough love.

I pray for better living arrangements. Where my monies are going toward purchasing a home, instead of paying my landlord's mortgage.

I pray for direction in making right choices concerning my relationships; I desire one that will ensure a powerful, loving, affectionate, respectful and trusting future.

I pray to learn to forgive myself for my own iniquities/sins. I must realize You are still here, regardless of my imperfections.

God please help me to change, so my consequences from choices are rewarding. Please remove my penalties from sin done, so that I may soar.

Take courage, son; your sins are forgiven and the penalty remitted.

Matthew 9:2b AMP

❧ Saying no to worldly desires, and yes to God is a challenging leap of faith. This is an important sign to discover where you are in your relationship with God. Once you are no longer being controlled by your flesh and its cravings, you have made way for your spirit to take control. At this time your desires will be God's desires. You will be walking in the perfect will that God has prepared for you since birth.

December 28, 2001 Noon

Confession of Faith (repeated every hour on the hour)

I do believe in the unseen.
I do believe in the unseen.
I do believe in the unseen.
I do believe in the unseen.
I call forth positive good results.
I call forth positive good results.
I call forth positive good results.
I call forth positive good results.
I do believe in the unseen.
I call forth positive good results.

<u>NOTES</u>: Taken from lessons at Unity, my home church.
<u>Faith</u>

"The law of use is the law of increase."
Seven Steps Toward Developing Faith:
1. Assent – agree with spiritual truths, "I'll try it"
2. Belief – believe "intellectually" the goodness of God
3. Conviction – the Divine assurance/developed

4. *Faith - believing in the Divine potential*
5. *Receptivity - listen to teachings of Jesus*
6. *Realization - conscious oneness*
7. *Trust - spiritual realization of truth*

At this point we turn into Christ's expression of faith.

I am receptive to Divine ideas. I accept the idea of my innate Divinity. I believe with all my thinking ability and faith, that I am God's perfect child. I trust God with all my heart. I identify with the all-conquering truth that I am a spiritual being, living in a spiritual universe governed by spiritual ideas.

For my thoughts are not your thoughts, neither are my ways your ways, saith the Lord. For as the heavens are higher than the earth, so are my ways higher than your ways, and my thoughts than your thoughts.

Isaiah 55:8-9

❧ In some cases we began to get to know God "intellectually." Meaning we get to know God through religion. This is only the first step towards developing your relationship with God, unfortunately many people stay in this place, where the knowledge is fed to them, and they seek no further. Religion is an education, but you need to put your education into practice. Our Spirit must grow with the Word of God found in the Bible. Seek the truth for yourself; not merely depending on the teaching of a qualified pastor/preacher. Philosophical truths about God bring on the intellectual knowledge of Him; revelation knowledge brings you into His presence. Revelation knowledge is when God can teach you one on one by His Word. God teaches His truths to your spirit. Man teaches God's truth to your Flesh. It is dangerous to substitute God's wisdom, for man's wisdom!

December 28, 2001   5:45 p.m. Near the End of Fast

God, I feel more faith. I envision a stable career, a beautiful home with plenty of room, a wonderful husband who loves You: the strength to stick with decisions I make. I will now stick to and believe all decisions I make come from "You." How can I doubt them? I must continue to have faith that all will turn out good.

Thank You for the visions that will be brought forth. Thank You for removing my penalties. I forgive myself for my iniquities/sins.

"Patience is the key, I will be anxious for nothing!"

I waited patiently and expectantly for the Lord; and He inclined to me and heard my cry. He drew me out of a horrible pit (a pit of tumult and of destruction), out of the miry clay (froth and slime), and set my feet upon a rock, steadying my steps and establishing my goings.

Psalms 40:1-2 AMP

❧ Today we can become overly anxious for things to happen in our lives. This is especially true when you are still trying to be part of a world that pleases all of your five senses (see, touch, taste, feel, and hear). Once you have chosen to walk closely to God (who is a Spirit and not of this world), having Him guide your way patience is truly the key to peace of mind. The truth that God reveals to you (once you recognize your spirit) can't be seen at first, but in time the truth and blessing you seek will be visible.

December 29, 2001   Saturday   Morning

Dear God,

I sat today going through pictures and old videotapes of acting jobs I'd done in Los Angeles.

I viewed a few, watched "E" television and suddenly felt the "desire" to become an actress again. To put my best foot forward and take what you send my *way. I've had these desires for several months now.*

Message from a few pastors I watched on religious channels:
"Let go and Let God."

I know my desires come from You, and I must put them into action. I'm praying for Your assistance, guidance, and for opportunities to become available. My desire is to be an actress for Your Glory. I did not have this desire before. Now I do.

Steps I must take:
Agent or agency
Head shots
Take classes
Utilize contacts in the industry

Before I formed you in the womb I knew (and) approved of you (as My chosen instrument), and before you were born I separated and set you apart, consecrating you; (and) I appointed you as a prophet to the nations.

Jeremiah 1:5 AMP

❦ "Let go and Let God" can be expressed by turning your will over to God, for His will, your destiny is already planned for your life. Let Him carry your burdens knowing that He loves you more than you could have ever imagined. By letting go and letting God guide your choices, you will experience the relief of pressure and aggravation as you find peace in Him. Entrust all outcomes to God who will not fail you like the world so often does.

December 29, 2001   4:15 p.m.

Dear God,

As I read the book of James, chapter one helped me to, "Stick to decisions made and bring them forth not wavering, not forcing anything, just letting it flow." I continue to hear this through prayer, and now from these readings I pray for the strength to stick to my decisions and not waver.

(For being as he is) a man of two minds (hesitating, dubious, irresolute), (he is) unstable and unreliable and uncertain about everything (he thinks, feels, decides).

James 1:8 AMP

✤ When we continue to change our minds from our first decisions, we have a tendency to not be taken seriously by others or ourselves. This opens the door to confusion, and God is not the author of confusion. When you send out conflicting thoughts, God is no longer able to manifest what is best for you because you are trying to assert your will over the situation. Make a decision to pray and open your self to the guidance God will send.

December 30, 2001   Sunday   Evening

Dear God,

I attended church with my best friend Sharon and her family along with my mom and her boyfriend, Darrell.

Wow, although I attend an awesome "truth" church that speaks primarily on the goodness of God, never have I been made so aware of the depths of satan and his presence in my life, and that it is he who presents bad things to us. God presents only good!

Be gone from my life satan, you have no more power! All my faith is with You, God! I will not let any anger, envy, jealousy, lack, limitation, or negativity enter my life any longer! I release the year 2001 and strive toward a great 2002! Next year will be God-filled; with His strength and faith He will supply all my needs and wants!

I gave an offering for being anointed (blessed with

more of God's wisdom) today at service; leaving my pockets depleted, but I know soon my prosperity and financial security will follow. Thank You in advance.

A truthful witness saves lives, but a deceitful witness speaks lies (and endangers lives).

Proverbs 14.25 AMP

The thief (satan) comes only in order to steal and to kill and destroy. I came that they may have and enjoy life, and have it in abundance (to the full, till it overflows).

John 10:10 AMP

❧ World doctrines will deceive us into believing that there is not an evil force in the spirit realm, therefore we war against each other. Satan is real. He comes to destroy the true plan that God has for your lives. He is the reason our soul is constantly at war with itself.

January 1, 2002   Tuesday   3:49 p.m.

Happy New Year God!

Thank You for this New Year filled with a new "awareness" of Your love. In the past several months of getting to know You through Your Word, I am also being exposed to my "real" self. I know I should be anxious for nothing, but I must say I'm a little, no, very excited to see how You will bring light to this darkness I am experiencing.

The darkness I'm experiencing has stemmed from a bunch of wrong choices: I'm currently unemployed due to a canceled contract; I need a new place to move into soon, because my lease is ending; My savings are reaching "empty;" My mother is living with me temporally; I'm in a relationship with a man who has two personalities, and I don't know what he does for a living; My other relationship of 5 years now with KG is on and off again, leaving me confused at times; I'm experiencing depression and I'm lonely even with tons of people around me.

My bedroom mirror reads, in red lipstick, Philippians 4:6-7:

"Be careful (anxious) for nothing; but in every thing by prayer and supplication with thanksgiving let your requests be made known unto God. And the peace of God, which passeth (surpasses) all understanding, shall keep (guard) your hearts and minds through Christ Jesus."

I was prompted, Father, to write this because I needed a daily reminder: No matter how things look on the outside, you have to be patient and trust in Your promises.

I'm so used to things happening so quickly in my life, but it's time for change, i.e., I have to wait to see my life turn for the better and let You show me what is in store for me.

My mom thinks she's driving me crazy, but You God know me best. Even in the midst of all this confusion and disappointment I am experiencing, I know I have a greater and holier challenge in front of me, that all my experiences are preparing me to walk with courage and faith in your Word. Your Spirit that lives within me has filled me with this knowledge and awareness. Thus, I can take myself to higher heights and put my desires to action.

God, I pray for balance this year. I know my year will be career-focused and self-focused, but I need the strength to make sure my time is spent wisely with family and friends. God, You being my number one focus and priority of course.

Your sun shall no more go down, nor shall your moon withdraw itself, for the Lord shall be your everlasting light, and the days of your mourning shall be ended.

Isaiah 60:20 AMP

I've experienced darkness, because I have been a people pleaser. Even as I was trying to walk with God I was self-focused, and still being a people pleaser. Self continues to block God from getting in all the way. I kept saying, "With the strength of God my desires will be put to action," but I'm still not letting Him in like He desires. I am now living to not please the world but to please myself. I have taken a step towards letting the Spirit truly come upon me. Eventually my flesh, my desire to control my life has to die. You too will come to a place in your life where you no longer look to the world to provide rather you turn to your self to provide stability and strength. This is only part of the process of living the life God has prepared for you, a life of peace as you walk in the Spirit.

January 2, 2002   Wednesday   Evening

Dear God,

Yet another "blessed," but challenging day. More debt arrived in the mail. Not enough money to pay them, but I know You God will fulfill all my needs. I know change is on the way! Soon! I will not wonder how.

I'm being anointed daily with this wonderful feeling of awareness and faith. You, God, have something in store for me. I feel chosen! I'm not scared either! Bring it on!

I do know I have to remove some distractions (worrying about my mother and brother's addictions; loneliness, even though I'm in a relationship; job security and financial stability) so that I may worship You more completely. I'm asking and praying to You for strength. I'm seeing darkness again, but I know the light will shine right on time. I'm learning daily from these struggles and pray that God when You do shine light upon me again, I will continue to praise and thank You daily, hourly, and by the minute. I'm tired of these valleys (going through the same things over and over). I want to give You, God all the attention and worship You deserve. I want to study more of Your Word (more of Your character and power) and find out exactly who I am in You. Nothing You have created should receive more attention then You!

Study to show thyself approved unto God, a workman that needeth not to be ashamed, rightly dividing the of truth.
2 Timothy 2:15

Here's a message I received for the second time, on this occasion it was while I attended service with my girlfriend Natasha at her Baptist church home ...

"I am going to have a good year with God being my number one priority."

Thank You God for continued awareness as I walk diligently seeking you.

The following are scriptures and notes taken:

But seek ye first the kingdom of God, and his righteousness; and all these things shall be added unto you. Matthew 6:33

❧ By following the Holy Spirit, we put our faith to action, allowing God to supply all our needs instead of relying on ourselves.

The number one goal is the desire to direct my affections and emotions towards God.

❧ God has made us for himself. He made things first so we wouldn't think we made things. He made you. You are not here for your own pleasure; you are here for God's pleasure. Even with my iniquities/sins God will not leave me. God, I will do my best to please You, so that You will please me. Thank You for letting me worship You!

"God tested Abraham with the offering of His son, this was only a test." Genesis 22:1-12

❧ Anything that takes too much of your time God will take it away! God is coming after everything You have placed in His spot, the G-spot (your heart).

Study to show thyself approved unto God, a workman that needeth not to be ashamed, rightly dividing the word of truth.

2 Timothy 2:15

❧ You can hear a powerful message from one of God's many vehicles (church, pastors, messengers), but if you do not study for yourself you will not have the interpretation from the greatest instructor, God as you read His Word, the scriptures meant just for your spiritual growth. Our flesh wants us to hear the Word and keep our Bible in the car after church service, and our spirit wants us to study the Word daily for our spiritual growth and awareness. The enemy can still influence your thoughts if you are only using the flesh to receive the Word. Hearing only, allows for too much room for confusion. This confusion is a tool satan uses. You need to be able to discern whom you are hearing from - God or satan.

January 3, 2002   Thursday   7:47 a.m.

Dear God,

Jesus said,
"Daughter, be of good comfort; thy faith hath made thee whole." Matthew 9:22

Thank You God for this comfort. Thank You God for forgiving me for my past sins. It's wonderful how You directed me to this verse. Thank You for showing me everything is okay.

Today I pray for guidance and good decision making concerning:
Meeting with a business associate for an independent contract in marketing. Is he sincere or not? Should I work with him?
[Answer: NO]

Meeting with Raymond (hometown friend). Bless our conversation and God bless his family.

Thank You God for Your patience, faith, and the following words:

"Worship not for blessings, but to show your thanks to God for being good to you."

"Whatever you give up, God will fill that void."

❧ God can and will speak to you through His Word, as you diligently seek Him and your heart truly desires His presence in your life.

January 5, 2002   Saturday   8:50 a.m.

Dear God,

Thank you for this day. Thank you for your wisdom and not mine. Thank you for helping me to get to know you like never before. This season of prayer is truly bringing me closer to you and to learning who I am. I am slowly recognizing my shortcomings because I now have time to re-evaluate my life. Thank You for your help. Wisdom from You defines who I should have been all this time (loving, gentle, faithful, honest and true).

Please bless the occurrences of this day. Please make me aware when needed. Guide me in conversation today. Please God, continue to prepare me for the good You are sending my way. Thank you. Bless Sharon (my best friend) and myself for completing her husband's presentation at church.

If any of you is deficient in wisdom, let him ask of the giving God (Who gives) to everyone liberally and ungrudgingly, without reproaching or faultfinding, and it will be given him.

James 1:5 AMP

January 6, 2002   Sunday   7:45 p.m.

Dear God,

Thank You for this thought: buy only videos you would want to be a character in one day. Study them, watch them for techniques and take notes of things to practice. Practice it, practice it, learn it, love it, and it will be all your heart's desire. I will never give you too much to handle. I know you will always praise Me.

The sheep that are My own hear and are listening to My voice; and I know them, and they follow Me.

John 10:27

✍ Was this really God speaking to me? Once again I did not have the power to discern whom I was hearing from yet. I was still in the midst of sin. As you move towards God, satan will present ideas and distractions to keep you where you are, in confusion lost to God's Divine purpose for you. But by questioning whom you are hearing from is a sign that you are becoming more aware of God in your life.

January 7, 2002   Monday   Morning

Dear God,

You want me to speak of my life, of how good You have been to me since I have come to sincerely desire to get to know You, and remove You from the box I had You in. I must let my light shine for others (non-believers), instead of trying to change them or preach the Word to them. Everyone needs love, everyone!

Thank You God, for making me aware as I study your Word (Your character and Your power) that I

41

must believe in the unseen; I must have faith. I know You are not of this world. The evil one has all these worldly things to tempt us, and he does this through our senses. They are visible; so many unbelievers rely on these things because it's easier. A true "challenge" is to believe in all things invisible. I can't see those things just yet. I will conquer that with Your guidance and strength, of course!

That no flesh should glory in his presence!

1 Corinthians 1:29

Most of us keep God in a box and only let Him out on Sunday's or when we need Him. God knows your heart. He wants to define who you truly are through His Word, but you have to desire this more than anything. You have learned to define yourself according to the world's value system and standards. Only God can reveal to you who you are, a child of God, a creation placed here to live in happiness, with peace, with the Holy Spirit within you.

You are here for God's Glory, not to please your flesh. It is God's desire for you to be a shining light for others that do not know Him and His goodness. There is no need to shine a searchlight on them, to shame them into knowing the Lord. Using only the light that is within is sufficient. Walking the walk will bring lost souls to want to get to know God, not merely talking the talk. It is through action and faith that true peace and purpose are blessed onto you.

Dear God,

Thank you for Your Word in the following scriptures: Depart from evil, and do good; and dwell forevermore (securely). Psalms 37:27

And the Lord shall help them, and delivers them (the righteous): he shall deliver them from the wicked, and save them, because they trust (and take refuge) in him. Psalms 37:40
Thank You God for this reading given to me by my mother. I've learned to listen more. I know it's not the messenger; it is the message.

Thank You for Your light God, patience is teaching me a lot. Good things come to those who wait.

Thank You God for my introductions to a few film contacts today. Thank You for Your will. Bless our meeting God. I pray to do a film produced by George Tillman since meeting him today. God, I pray for a character in his current production." Thank You, please use me!

Wait and hope for and expect the Lord; be brave and of good courage and let your heart be stout and enduring. Yes, wait for and hope for and expect the Lord.

Psalms 27:14 AMP

❧ God blesses us with His will not ours, once you surrender and die to self (worldly desires)! I still had not completely surrendered yet, so I was still being deceived and trying to walk in my will though thinking it was His. It takes time for self/flesh to submit to the Spirit, where it belongs.

January 9, 2002   Wednesday   7:45 a.m.

I pray that everything is okay with Mark; I'm very concerned and am having horrible visions about him being in some sort of trouble. I don't know exactly what he does for a living and 12 years ago, I had a similar relationship that ended in death. Over the past few days, he's been quite busy with his associates, but still communicates and laughs with me. He keeps telling me to stay focused while pushing me (supporting me) to get my picture ready for this casting director.

I talked to him yesterday several times before his 2 p.m. appointment. I was busy for a while myself, and I didn't call him until about 6 p.m. No answer, so I left a message. I called again close to 10 p.m.; no answer, no call back. It's now tomorrow, and I'm concerned. He's always been very good in communicating with me ... this isn't normal. I feel that something isn't right. Please keep him safe, let me be wrong this time. God, please lift my worries and let me know everything is okay. I trust in You. Thank You.

So God created man in his own image, in the image of God created he him; male and female created he them.

Genesis 1:27

🌿 God is saying, "Will you please focus on Me as much as you focus on one of My creations? I'm trying to reveal to you life instead of death."

🌿 It is also through visions/dreams that God reveals signs as to potential dangers in your path or distractions that satan is creating especially for you. It is not until the next day that I realize my thoughts about Mark are hindering my walk, but I am still not seeing the signs God is sending me.

January 9, 2002   5:30 p.m.

Dear God,

Please forgive me for the last entry in my journal. Please forgive me for giving so much attention to someone who cannot fill my every desire as You can. I know I must focus on my number one priority, You. All things will flow at that moment. I know my choices create my present and future. I pray for the strength to make the right ones. I know You give me signs and by choice sometimes I don't take heed to Your signs. I pray for strength, I pray for Your light and Your understanding. Please be patient with me.

Wisdom is the principal thing; therefore get wisdom: and with all thy getting get understanding.

Proverbs 4:7

Love is what we are created of (once born again). I want to discover what is within me. Thank You for love, thank You for answered prayer, thank You for always being on time.

Lift me from my doubts and confusion. Guide me. My heart desires what Your will is for me. Give me strength to make the choices that align with Your will. And so it is, Amen.

This book of the Law (the Bible) shall not depart out of your mouth, but you shall meditate on it day and night, that you may observe and do according to all that is written in it. For then you shall make your way prosperous, and you shall deal wisely and have good success. Joshua 1:8

I call heaven and earth to witness this day against you that I have set before you life and death, the blessings and the curses; therefore choose life, that you and your descendants may live.

Deuteronomy 30:19 AMP

✱ The Bible is your way to understanding how to experience Heaven on earth, you don't have to wait to get there! "Heaven on earth" is a present by God and "Hell on earth" is a present with a bomb in it by satan. The Bible is your guide to life or death. It's your choice!

<u>January 10, 2002</u>   **Thursday**   <u>10 p.m.</u>

Dear God,

Thank You for a day in which I felt like I was flowing. I didn't force anything to happen. It was a great feeling.

I've received advice from several of Your messengers (pastors, teachers, preachers, friends, and strangers) who showed me what I need to focus on; what I want for myself not on my relationships, or how I can please others. I paid close attention to the things I focused and spoke on throughout the day. My focus was not on You, God, my number one source. It should be on You, so that I may not miss anything You have for me some awareness You want me to acknowledge. Opportunities are coming my way, but You, God, know my heart's desire. It's true, I do desire a position with this prosperous wireless company as their marketing director, but only if it is Your will. I feel in my heart that it's okay by You to want this position because I have let go and prayed for Your guidance and will in receiving it. Please allow the deadline date to be met so I can continue my 2002 career focus.

I'm trying God to learn and understand life; please bring the light. Thank You.

Let be and be still, and know (recognize and understand) that I am God, I will be exalted among the nations! I will be exalted in the earth!

Psalms 46:10 AMP

❧ I did not have the knowledge of Christ; I knew something was in me. With this in mind, I had not sat still long enough to let God direct me in His way. I was still trying to make something happen like I've done in the past. I was still trying to control my destiny. I stated that I let go, but not all the way. God's guidance is presenting Itself, but not His perfect will because my "self" was still getting in the way. You will come to a point where you will no longer feel as though you must control your life, your faith will be so strong in the Lord that all decisions are automatically placed in His hands.

❧ If you have been titled as a control freak, Jesus is the answer! He will reverse that curse!

<u>January 11, 2002</u>   Friday   11:45 p.m.

Dear God,

I must say, I'm learning to feel confident and stable with my choices. I'm learning to be stern when making a point concerning something I believe. I'm learning to let You guide my day. When I do this, it's nothing but peaceful. No stress, nothing confuses me; not one worldly thing gets too much of my attention because I know I must remain aware so as not to miss the next step or word You have for me. God I want victory. I want Your light to be able to shine on others. This is the best feeling of security I've ever had. I will not lose this love from You.

I have no job, no income, but still You come when I need You, right on time - bills paid on time. Thank You. I planted and sowed a seed (an offering) tonight at church, and I know my prosperity is about to overflow.

I understand that this is my season to pray and be still, that's why work is not coming so easily like usual. Next season will be used to my newly acquired strength. Thank You, God.

To everything there is a season, and a time for every matter or purpose under heaven...He has made every thing beautiful in its time.

Ecclesiastes 3:1,11 AMP

❧ It's always the season to pray. God will cause you to be still by removing a job or a relationship in order to force you to be alone with yourself and Him. You must pray without ceasing. The strength then becomes always available to you, not just for a season. All things of the world are in seasons, but all that is of God of the supernatural are never changing, always present. There was more power for me to encounter; I was not aware of this just yet. When a situation arises that at first looks like a loss of something important to the flesh, you need to realize God is reaching out to you. He is presenting an opportunity for you to quiet the "worldly you" in preparation for your next level spiritually. It may be something as simple as losing a job or as impacting as going to prison. Remain aware of why certain worldly things are taken away ... God is trying to bring you to Him, to save you from a world influenced by satan.

January 12, 2002   Saturday   8:04 p.m.

Dear God,

Thank You for my friends. Thank You for continued awareness of my self and especially the choices being presented to me everyday. Thank You for giving me the ability to turn a negative into a positive. You blessed me with a great vision today. Thank You.

Here's the vision:
± Record spiritual thoughts on a tape recorder
± Get thoughts put on tape from my pocket p.c.
± Get producer to put music to Your words (very unique)
± Do music video with exotic look, speaking those words and thoughts
Benefit:
± Uplift those who seek peace
± Speak of God through soulful words & soulful tunes
± Market will encompass all ethnicities
Put these steps to action

For the desires of the flesh are opposed to the Holy Spirit, and the Spirit are opposed to the flesh (godless human nature) for these are antagonistic to each other, continually in conflict with one another, so that you are not free but are prevented from doing what you desire to do.

Galatians 5:17

❧ I was still hitting a joint periodically at this time. I don't know if this was God or satan talking to me. It's so important to learn how to live in the spirit realm, because when you are in the fleshly things of the world, you do not know who is giving you all these great ideas. I learned if it didn't manifest, it was not of God. His perfect will is all I want. As you move closer to God, you will become more mindful of the choices and consequences of each choice. Regret and sin will sit heavily within you, your self will wage war with your spirit because you realize there is better meant for you.

January 13, 2002   Sunday   12:26 p.m.

Dear God,

Thank You for Helice Green, the Pastor of Unity Church. Thank You for the love and peace I received during service. I realize daily when I hear Your message for the day, that I'm already aware of the words to be spoken. I realize the Word is always there; that God is always within.

I continue to receive confirmation on how you should stick to choices and ideas made. Believe them, have faith in the manifestation of them, and all will be good, great, and prosperous.

I sizzle with delight when I wake up in the morning to be used again in God's wonderful plan. I set my human self aside and let God guide my spirit.

For everyone who continues to feed on milk is obviously inexperienced and unskilled in the doctrine of righteousness (of conformity to the divine will in purpose, thought, and action), for he/she is mere infant (not able to talk yet)!But solid food is for full-grown men/women, for those whose senses and mental faculties are trained by practice to discriminate and distinguish between what is morally good and noble and what is evil and contrary either to divine or human law.

Hebrews 5:12 AMP

God is preparing me for my next level of spiritual knowledge at this church. My foundation has been laid here. I am being fed the milk of His Word like a newborn baby being nursed at this point. Eventually as a believer, your Spirit will no longer desire to be hand-fed but will hunger and thirst to search out the truth by reading the Word for your own understanding, therefore created a craving for more and more. Your Spirit will desire a church that teaches on more than just one scripture and the philosophical viewpoints of a man. Your Spirit will urge you to desire a message that is taught from the Bible; scripture to scripture; a Word church. A church where the teacher is led by the Holy Ghost sharing the reality of the Bible and who you are in Christ. At this time your Spirit can grow with the meat of the Word. Your Spirit wants to advance from being a child to being a son/daughter of God. It will be your choice to move when your Spirit says move. Sometimes you may fear what is to come because of the comfort zone of where you are, but knowing more of the truth, and getting to really know Jesus can open your eyes to the true darkness you may be living in.

<u>January 14, 2002</u>　　　Monday　　　Morning

Good morning God,

I pray for a day filled with Your will for me. God, I desire to live right by You in all ways, especially when it comes to sex. I just want what You have for me. Give me strength and wisdom to make the right choices. Bless my meeting today with the wireless company. May Your will be done.

I love You God. Thank You for making me realize I'm never alone. I'll always have You. Bless my mother today; bring her the light. Thank You, I appreciate, have faith in, and believe in You.

Please Lord, please God bless me with the finances to secure my transportation. Thank You.

Shun immorality and all sexual looseness (flee from impurity in thought, word, or deed). Any other sin, which a man commits, is one outside the body, but he who commits sexual immorality sins against his own body. Do you not know that your body is the temple (the very sanctuary) of the Holy Spirit Who lives within you, Whom you have received (as a gift from God? You are not your own, you were bought with a price (purchased with a preciousness and paid for, made His own). So then, honor God and bring glory to Him in your body.

1 Corinthians 6:18 AMP

My true struggles and challenges before knowing Jesus Christ were men (not being able to do without one), sex (not being able to do without it, and using it to control others), and finances (debt knocked at my door no matter how much money I was making). I just couldn't seem to manage it. I was caught in curses that were not part of God's plan. Like many believers, I have remained comfortable (out of fear of the unknown) to remain only hearing the Word thus satan still has access to my weaknesses, mainly sex and men. You must continue to move along your path, do not fear what you cannot see or control, God will replace all your fleshy desires once you take it upon yourself to understand the reality of His Word. Fear is death, it is of satan. Faith is life, it is God manifested within you.

January 14, 2002   4:55 p.m.

God,

Please bless me with this acting opportunity with MGM that's surfaced. If it's Your will God let me get a call to come in and let me "fall" the way they want me to as it states in the script. I pray for and desire this chance should You desire it for me. I will be patient and wait.

Be anxious for nothing ... Be anxious for nothing ... Be anxious for nothing. All good things come from God.

Thank You, God. Please take this curse off me; this need to talk rather than listen. Silence is the key to receiving you. I'm learning to do my best when it comes to being slow-to-speak. I keep trying to share my walk with non-believers who do not have an ear to hear. My boyfriend is a non-believer.

And He answered them, O unbelieving generation (without any faith)! How long shall I (have to do) with you? How long am I to bear with you? Bring him to Me.

St. Mark 9:19 AMP

✌ Non-believers of your faith may not have an ear to hear the good message you are trying to share with them. Stop! If it seems difficult, challenging, and turns into a debate. It's obviously not up to you to plant that seed. Especially if it is an ex-boyfriend/girlfriend! Just know, as God has been successful in getting His message to you of his "realness," He surely can get the message to the non-believers in your midst. Once we are saved, it is not our first assignment to save the world. We are to be focused on becoming who we are in Christ. We need to minister to ourselves (the Christ in us), then others. Our light will bring lost souls to God. You better believe God knows what He's doing! Get out of the way!!

January 14, 2002   Monday   5:55 p.m.

Dear God,

You are the only source I know I can communicate with who understands me. Only You can judge me. I sit here on the couch and as I watch my mother on the computer working hard creating poetry, I love her more than she will ever know. All the prosperity and desires I pray for in the long run will make it possible for me to get my mother the things she needs. I know we have to be individuals, and she should be *able to have the things she needs and desires through faith. But deep inside God, I want to be able to help my mom as much as You allow me to.*

Bless her and put her in Your light. Thank You.

Now to Him Who, by (in consequence of) the (action of His) power that is at work within us, is able to (carry out His purpose and) do superabundantly, far over and above all that we (dare) ask or think (infinitely beyond our highest prayers, desires, thoughts, hopes, or dreams)—To Him be glory in the church and in Christ Jesus throughout all generations forever and ever. Amen (so be it).

Ephesians 3:20-21 AMP

❧ You may feel it is your responsibility to provide for those you love, but through prayer and not necessarily always material blessings you can give the greatest gift of all, the gift of God (Love). God is our source and He always comes right on time. Remember the saying, "He may not come when you want Him to, but He is always right on time!" This is the truth if you believe it. Trust and rely on the Lord your God.

January 15, 2002   Tuesday   3:15 p.m.

Dear God,

I've just read Matthew 13 (all verses) and pray to sow seeds on good soil only. Soil that presently bears good fruit. I pray for Your great presence and precious will for my life. Thank You for answers, thank You for the chance to build a foundation again. Thank You for the time to spend with You, as I have not secured employment yet. You have made me "still" for a reason. Thank You for showing me how great it is to learn, live, and be in Your presence always. I know and accept Your plan for my life. If I don't receive something prayed for, I accept that it is not Your will, or it is not Your timing. Thank You for the time to study the Word once again.

Study to show thyself approved unto God, a workman that needeth not to be ashamed, rightly dividing the word of truth.

2 Timothy 2:15

I pray for Your will and guidance with the wireless company, and also with an associate named Veronica who's in the market for an actress and a marketing consultant for a play production she wrote. We are meeting so she may present this to me. I love You and appreciate You.

As for what was sown on good soil, this is he who hears the Word and grasps and comprehends it; he indeed bears fruit and yields in one case a hundred times as much as was sown in another sixty time as much, and in another thirty.

Matthew 13:23 AMP

✒ When we plant seeds, invest our thoughts and actions in any particular person or event, you must choose to lay your seed on soil that is bearing good fruit. Surround yourself with people of God, with opportunities that build your faith. Though Jesus sat with the sinners it was because He was filled with the Holy Spirit. Until the Holy Spirit comes upon you, it is important to not plant yourself on ground-bearing thorns, offering sin. You may not be able to discern this.

January 17, 2002   Thursday   7:50 a.m.

Dear God,

What would You have me do today? This morning I woke up in darkness feeling lonely and a little lost.

Things do not seem to be moving fast enough. Please God show me the light. Please. This is my prayer. I love You.

Casting down imaginations, and every high thing that exalteth itself against the knowledge of God and bringing into captivity every thought to the obedience of Christ.

2 Corinthians 10:5

❧ When you are accustomed to controlling every aspect of your life, it is difficult to sit idle while you wait for God to bring you His message and direction. It is now, that you build your faith through prayer and acceptance of what will come in its due time.

❧ Satan plants impatience and worry in your mind; you must cast away doubt. Cast satan out!

Janaury 17, 2002   5:45 p.m.

Dear God,

Just knowing that I'm one with You, my spirits are lightened. I know I can't look at my outer circumstances, because I may see darkness (financial lack, rejection with past and present employment and con-

*fusing relationships). I must stay tuned to my inner
self for peace, that's who I am. What a wonderful
thing! I embrace Your kingdom within me.*

Arise (from the depression and prostration in which circumstances have kept you—rise to a new life)! Shine (be radiant
with the glory of the Lord), for your light has come, and the
glory of the Lord has risen upon you!

Isaiah 60:1 AMP

≈ The only way for you to confront darkness is to admit that
you are lost. Above I stated that I "might" see darkness, what
belongs there is I "will" see darkness. It's a reality, as you
become more familiar with Jesus, delight when you face challenges because you will know that it is the Christ within you (the
anointing) that makes satan's attempts clear and visible. At this
time the darkness will be an opportunity for you to move further
into God's light.

January 17, 2002   9:40 p.m.

Dear God,

*I must apologize to You, and I know You forgive me.
I am sorry that at the age of 33 I'm just realizing
You are All and have always been here. I sit here
crying out of happiness, out of a sense of under-*

standing as I sit and listen to the trials and outcomes of people around me, the ones who walk in faith.

It is we who make life choices, putting money, work and relationships before You God, which leads to disappointments, sadness and suffering. With all of this time, we could have had the opposite: the positive, the good, and no drama – Jesus. But I guess my experiences and hearing others has brought me to a point of wanting Your promises. Only these promises are good.

At the end of age 32, after seeing things are not going the way "I" planned for them ... my career, my relationships (I would end one for another), and family problems (drugs, lack and dependency), I had to step aside and finally let You take control.

Why did I have to find out so late?

I keep asking myself, but it's never too late for God to work in my life and make it all He wants it to be. I just had to let Him. I changed my name back to its original spelling to take back my true identity. (In Los Angeles, while pursuing acting, I changed it to

Trayce because that was the thing to do). I'm learning to be alone for God and for me time. I'm more responsible. I don't live for the world. I'm praying for the desires of my heart in solitude and in sacred places.

I'm ready for the new Tracy; someone I always knew was there. No more of the worldly Trayce.

I want to and pray to see good in all situations. I actually have been experiencing this and its great results. I'm learning to accept others for who they are and know that they are still on a journey just as I am. I'm learning to stick to my decisions after consulting with God.

"But seek ye first the kingdom of God, and his righteousness; and all these things shall be added unto you." Matthew 6:33

This is a true challenge, but day-by-day as I become more aware, it's turning into the best focus I could ever have. Just loving God and knowing He has always been with me, after having a heart of repentance. Even realizing my iniquities and admitting *them to Him, now all else will fall into place!*

(What, what would have become of me) had I not believed that I would see the Lord's goodness in the land of the living! Wait and hope and expect the Lord; be brave and of good courage and let your heart be stout and enduring. Yes, wait for and hope and expect the Lord.

Psalms 27:13-14 AMP

❧ You need to realize that it's your wrong thinking and choices that causes disappointment, suffering and loss in your life. It is up to you to turn to God first, to learn from past consequences, and look this day forward to Him when making decisions. Go to God with everything. He will help you pick out the perfect pair of shoes, or the designer suit that is now half off. Oh yeah, He will guide you to some deals! Once you see that God has your best interest in mind, because you are His child, you will not want to turn from Him. When you make mistakes, you will only run closer to Him and His "agape" (unconditional) Love for you. His mercy will stay with you as a believer forever. Where would we be without Him? ... In the dust.

January 20, 2002   Sunday   12:50 p.m.

All praises to the almighty God!

This day is filled with positive affirmations, from my

morning prayer to my spiritual tapes in the car and finally from my Unity Church service. Thank You God for a positive day. I didn't know God that "I" can shape and mold my life. I can and will do it gracefully with Your constant guidance. I feel good advising You on all of my next steps. I have let go and let You lead my way.

I feel so secure knowing and believing in the unseen; knowing and believing more is in store for me, in receiving the desires of my heart. To live for You! My imagination is going from acting, to dancing, to taking the marketing world to higher heights. First, I had to pray for and see Your light, then I had to have faith. With the knowing that I recognize both, You have my imagination running! I know what I picture I can have. I must always remember that it is through You. I must remember to pray and meditate on this. It's amazing how the doors are going to open.

Thank You God.

For the Word that God speaks is alive and full of power (making it active, operative, energizing, and effective); it is sharper than any two-edged sword, penetrating to the dividing line of the breath of life (soul) and (the immortal) spirit, and of joints and marrow (of the deepest parts of our nature), exposing and sifting and analyzing and judging the very thoughts and purposes of the heart.

Hebrews 4:12 AMP

🌿 I had not yet prayed for God's "perfect" Will. It was still all about my "permissible" will and me, but I was not aware of this just yet. What is happening and what you must do is believe in the unseen and speak it as a truth in your life. Then it will be manifested through the Holy Spirit working with you as you put things to action as you are led.

🌿 Your heart must be pure and cleansed to experience the character of God. You have to sacrifice what you have been educating your mind with and start the renewing process with things that will keep reminding you of the goodness of God (the Word, teachings, spiritual music and fellowship with other believers). Affirmations are great, and they build a positive foundation, but God's Word is His character and His power. It will penetrate your heart with the reality of it just by reading it (even if you don't understand it yet). It will walk you to another level God wants you to be in.

Dear God,

May Your will be done today in this life You have blessed me with. Please let there be light. I have a part of me that misses Mark, (we haven't communicated for about a week and we don't know why), and I miss talking to him. I have another side of me that can't deal with his lack of happiness. I know our relationship will soon end because we're not on the same page. When that time comes, God, please let Your will be done in the conversation. Is he the man for me or not?

I was given the book, The Prayer of Jabez; thank You for having it put in my life. I will pray this prayer daily with my meditation or during my prayer.

"Oh God bless me, bless me indeed. Oh God enlarge my territory. Oh God that Your hand be with me, and God please keep evil from me." Thank You.

I appreciate, adore, love, respect, honor, and breathe You God.

The Lord is far from the wicked, but He hears the prayer of the (consistently) righteous (the upright, in right standing with Him).

Proverbs 15:29 AMP

✄ The Prayer of Jabez is a bold request for God to move in your life. This is God's Word and His will for you. If you are sincerely seeking God and the reality of His Word your soul will be blessed inside first then outside. You will receive all that you have prayed for according to His will. If you pray for your own will, you just may get it, and believe me, there will be a lesson in it. When it's all said and done, you will end up right back where you started; seeking God's will for your life.

January 23, 2002   Wednesday   9:20 a.m.

Dear God,

Thank You for this day You have blessed me with! Oh God bless me, bless me indeed, enlarge my territory, oh that Your hand will be with me and keep me from evil. Thank You for Your goodness. Please busy me God today with Your will. What can I do today to fulfill Your will?

I must give a testimony... I haven't secured a job yet,

but I prayed and asked You that when my car reached 46,000 miles that I would be able to afford my maintenance and brake job. You have blessed me at 45,933 miles to afford to fix both. The maintenance was less money than I had thought, and I was told that my brakes didn't need to be fixed at this time. Thank You, God, for adding an additional 7,500 miles to my brakes.

I pray God, for a blessing of a home or condo by March 1. I have to leave my current residence because it's going on the market or work it out for me to stay where I am through a home loan. Please bless my mother's efforts in finding a home also.

Thank You God. I wait patiently!

And my God will liberally supply (fill to the full) your every need according to His riches in glory in Christ Jesus.

Philippians 4:19 AMP

✄ At this moment I was learning how to let God supply my every need. He was showing me that I could depend on Him, and stop looking to man when I needed financial assistance. You must believe enough in God to turn your concerns and problems over to Him. Have faith and patience and if you stay aware He will deliver your need, a messenger and/or sign to guide you.

January 24, 2002   Thursday   Morning

Dear God,

Thank You for yesterday's impulse to go visit my brother in jail. This brought both my mom and me peace of mind. A peaceful drive it was. My brother was shocked and happy. Thank You for love. Thank You for family love.

During the drive God, I received a revelation to keep my focus on knowing and feeling comfortable with what You have in store for me in Your time. Sometimes, when I can't see the light, I let other things bother me like people, situations, and the world, but just receiving a sense of comfort from You was a spiritual high. I realized nothing of the world could take my joy away. This is the joy of knowing and believing in the unseen. Thank You for Your wisdom. Thank You for bringing the light every time I need it. I have to know that it's there all the time for me to receive. It's my choice.

Thank You for things moving forward with the marketing opportunity I prayed for. With Your hand with me, I will begin "due diligence" in regards to the wireless company. I love You, God.

Since we consider and look not to the things that are seen but to the things that are unseen; for the things that are visible are temporal (brief and fleeting), but the things that are invisible are deathless and everlasting.   2 Corinthians 4:18 AMP

And when the devil had ended every (the complete cycle of) temptation, he (temporarily) left Him (that is, stood off from Him) until another more opportune and favorable time.

Luke 4:13 AMP

✍ Believing in the unseen is the ultimate act of faith. Satan will continue to place distraction in front of you, i.e. finances, partners, stress, all in an attempt to test and break your faith.

January 27, 2002   Sunday   8:29 a.m.

Good morning God,

I praise and adore You. I anticipate learning more about You. I prayed for a great memory so I can

minister Your Word to those who ask.

Bless my girlfriend in L.A., Latasha. Thank You for the words of encouragement and spiritual uplifting I was able to minister to her. She was wondering why her life goes up and down? Why her plans never succeed? I told her it's not your life! It's God's! Get to know the Creator of your life, and He will guide You to His plan especially prepared just for You. You just have to step aside and give Him permission. Let the Holy Spirit, sent by Jesus Christ, work through You.

Jesus answered and said unto him, Verily, verily, I say unto thee, Except a man be born again, he cannot see the kingdom of God.

John 3:3

For the Holy Spirit to come and live within you; you must have a sincere heart of repentance, confessing your sins out loud to God (not man) and accepting Jesus as your Lord and Savior. You must be cleansed of your sins by the blood of Jesus to be Born-again!

Oh God bless me, bless me indeed! Enlarge my territory God. Oh, that Your hand be with me and keep evil from me. Thank You.

I look forward to my service today, to deliver Your message with my Pastor. I ask to receive knowledge from the words.

January 27, 2002   3:50 p.m.

Dear God,

I don't want to get to heaven and find out about all these blessings on earth that I missed because I wanted my will and not Yours. I continue to pray daily for Your will. Make me aware so I will not miss any goodness and blessings You send me. So many of us receive only one of Your blessings (a creative thought, impulse, insight, emotion etc.) daily when You probably have 20 or more for us. I want mine!

✥ "The Prayer of Jabez" book is really making me bolder in prayer and requests, but that's not what getting to know God is all about. What I found most important is to worship and tell God, at all times, how much you love Him. Then make requests if you desire. He already knows them anyway, before you ask, but you must still speak them aloud.

January 28, 2002 Monday 2:59 p.m.

Dear God,

Thank You for the changes in my life. Changes have occurred in my attitude towards life. I'm being more positive in all that I do. Also, I've been doing my best to make the right decisions for more rewarding, peaceful results for myself. I know these changes are Your doing, and that they are making way for the good to come from You.

The career opportunity with the wireless company is in Your hands; bless me with it if it's Your will. (I have not secured this position yet).

Bless Mark, I've realized after so many conversations and signs, that yes, I have some things to work on and change in me, but he is not sent by You. I have to stop trying to be a people pleaser. I have to listen and respect their wishes. To give them what they want, not what I think they need. For instance, Mark told me not to buy him a birthday cake, but I ignored the request disregarding his reason for not wanting to celebrate. (He lost his parents around the same time that his birthday falls).

Bless my mother, may she have a great day at work.
I love her, God; please forgive me for any disrespect
I show toward her due to her backsliding into drug use
now and throughout my life. I have been angry,
resentful, and closed-off to her at times. Please heal
me and teach me to show love no matter what.

Now am I trying to win the favor of men, or of God? Do I seek to please men? If I were still seeking popularity with men, I should not be a bond servant of Christ (the Messiah).

Galatians 1:10 AMP

✣ I continue to find that satan uses those that are very close and dear to your heart to try to take you away from God's presence. It's usually your family members that can prompt you to be the old you or you that is not of God. This is an attempt that all should be aware of. Regardless of the person or situation present at any moment, you must stay true to who you are, which is a son and daughter of love, compassion, patience and acceptance. Do not allow distractions to change whom you are at heart, who in God's image we were made.

January 28, 2002   10:05 p.m.

Dear God,

This day was obviously filled with several challenges.
I woke feeling lonely, my money is getting low, I

haven't found a stable career, and my move-out date is soon approaching. Mom is using again, and it pains me to see her so out of touch with the world and God.

These challenges did not break me. God brought me light on each, His peace because I asked. It only took one day for me to find satisfaction in the inner peace I'd been experiencing, even if victory had not come.

Thank You God for loving me.

For though the mountains should depart and the hills be shaken or removed, yet My love and kindness shall not depart from you, nor shall My covenant of peace and completeness be removed says the Lord, Who has compassion on you.

Isaiah 54:10 AMP

❧ You must be able to detach at some point, by stepping back and allowing God's patience and will to work through you. Accept the situation or relationship as it is and just know that change and peace are coming. God's peace will overcome any trial and pain satan presents.

January 29, 2002   Tuesday   11:00 a.m.

Dear God,

You never cease to protect me from making the same wrong choices that tend to shape a future that is not from You. I know You have something in store for me that You will not let me miss. I feel it. Keep helping me to remove negativity out of my life. You have my permission to continue working in and through me. I have faith in Your outcome not mine any longer.

I will not give up on seeking Your goodness. I will be patient, wait and listen. I look forward to telling my testimony.

Thank You for opening the communication barriers between my mother and me. I love her and need her.

May Your will be done. Protect me from going back to where I was.

"Oh God bless me, bless me indeed. Oh, that You enlarge my territory. Keep Your hand with me and keep me from evil." I appreciate You.

🌿 I know I am being prepared for a purpose because the situations and obstacles I face are building my faith and resolve in God. There is a purpose behind everything we come into contact with, knowing this is the key to surviving and living the life God has destined for you.

January 29, 2002   9:25 p.m.

Dear God,

I feel You. You most definitely have a protective shield over me. I pray for light, You bring me light. I pray for financial support, and You send me a check in the mail. I pray for answers to concerns. When I'm patient, I receive my answers.

You continue to save me. It's like You have me on hold for something special. You are using me and saving me for something special, I know it! It's finally my turn or should I say it's finally time to receive Your good plan for me. You have taught me over the years and finally I accept the "Truth." I'm aware of You being here within me! I feel and know all I have to do is follow You and let You guide me.

I've lost my relationship, a place to live, no job, and all things worldly that could get the best of someone who doesn't know Your goodness. I know all things have happened for a reason. I'm being prepared for major change, Your change. All because I asked for it!

I know You will send me a caring, good-spirited, soulful relationship, because I asked You.

I know You will send me opportunities for a better place for my mom and me to live, because I asked You.

I know I will be able to tell my aspiring actress story because I asked You.

I know You will continue to provide for me financially, because I asked You.

Whatever Your will is, I ask for it. You're making changes in my life for my good. I wait patiently, without being upset as change occurs. Please continue to do Your thing! I invite You! This is the best feeling in my life. I feel so safe. I finally have a Father who will always love me!

🌿 After we have done all that we can, we will always come to a point of desiring what God would have for us to do in this life "HE" blessed us with. The problem is, "precious time" is utilized as you come to realize that God's way is the only way. Spiritual knowledge is the key.

February 3, 2002   Sunday   Morning

Dear God,

Forgive me from the bottom of my heart. I've been in Florida visiting KG (my best friend and ex-boyfriend) and slipped into sexual sin. I need Your strength to know that I will not punish myself. Please let me know. Please show me that You are still preparing a wonderful plan for me. I repent! Thank You for loving me regardless of my iniquities/sins.

🌿 As you become more aware of sin, when you fall the consequence will be small in comparison to the conviction you place upon yourself. You will be so tender to the idea of sinning that it becomes less and less frequent.

As I look through my journal pages, I see blurred spots. My tears stain the pages, reminding me of choices I've made in my life that I punish myself with. I must learn that I can choose to be happy or sad. I choose to be happy, knowing that in all things I have You, and You will show me the light always, even if I created darkness. Thank You. I strive to be this "Proverb 31 woman": strong, respected, stable, and secure. Until marriage, I need and pray for the strength to be this woman for You, God, then my earth-husband. Make me, mold me into this woman. I invite You to work in and through me God.

Thank You God for the times You grant me to speak of You. Thank You for a good listener. Bless KG with his good intentions of finding You. May he grow in Your Word and grow out of this world. Will we be friends in the spirit forever? Anything else that may be a result of our friendship let it be Your will.

🌿 Although I had become aware of the spirit within me and getting stronger daily in God's Word, I still did not have enough wisdom about the deceitfulness wanting me to leave God's presence. I did not have the power of discernment. Satan was attempting to keep me with a guilty conscious and it was winning. More of God's wisdom and gifts was the answer.

Oh yeah, I wanted to thank you again for a past blessing : Last month I prayed to have enough money to pay for my brakes and my service mainte-nance. At this time, I didn't know how it would hap-pen, but I kept the faith. This was going to be required at 46,000 miles, which was soon approaching. Within a week my car reached those miles and you blessed me with the resources to pay. Also to my amazement my brakes went from 2% left on them to having 50% more to go, therefore I ended up not needing a brake job. Thanks again God!

Study to show thyself approved unto God, a workman that needeth not to be ashamed, rightly dividing the word of truth.

2 Timothy 2:15

My people are destroyed for lack of knowledge: because thou hast rejected knowledge ...

Hosea 4:6a

I was continuously depending on God to supply my every need through prayer and faith. Studying His Word daily was opening my eyes to the realization He only wants the best for me. Also, I am to call on Him for all things, not just some things – all things.

Dear God,

I just have to give You praise! Once again, I experienced being used by You. I was able to minister/speak of Your Word while visiting KG when I missed my 7:25 a.m. flight because a young guy was so persistent in speaking to me; he would not take no for an answer. I didn't feel like being bothered, but he just wouldn't give up. Long story short, we spoke of Your Word, and I was able to minister to him. He listened earnestly and appreciated the words, which flowed directly from You. He has just begun his search for his purpose and realized after speaking to me that You are the answer. All he had to do was listen and ask. I showed him Matthew 13:12 which speaks on spiritual knowledge:

For whosoever hath [spiritual knowledge], to him shall be given, and he shall have more abundance: but whosoever hath not [spiritual knowledge], from him shall be taken away even that he hath.

He thanked me and said, "I never would have known that by sitting down just to bother you that I would *end up being spiritually good. Thank You."*

Thank You for using me God. I look forward to my next opportunity to minister and share your truth.

And I will make of thee a great nation, and I will bless thee, and make thy name great; and thou shall be a blessing:

Genesis 12:2

❧ Spiritual knowledge far surpasses all else. Our sprirt grows from God's truth, His Word, the Bible.

February 3, 2002   Revelation

God, I jotted down thoughts that You brought to my attention to share in a letter to KG, who cares for me tremendously, but seems reluctant to get closer, because of some of my family challenges, instead of seeing me for who I truly am.

Here it goes:
I may not come from a family of riches and good-ness, but... I come from God, a Father of riches and goodness. I am His strong child.

Who are You to judge me by my life, by my family members, by my character in this world?

I am a seeker of God, a seeker of a true, happy, good spirit. These are all the riches I desire. He will give me all of these unworldly desires and what I need and want on this earth.

If my spirit and heart are of the goodness and strength of God, surely all will prevail.

Can you not see past my outer and know it's my inner self you love the most? That I love the most. All I can do is love You with an everlasting love and that is truly all I desire of You, nothing more and most definitely nothing less.

God at birth placed me with a family that would only make me stronger in years to come. He is now showing me that I have been blessed and will be soon rewarded for letting Him use me. Now is my new journey, a journey of inward self-definition.

Spiritual beauty plus outer beauty is a true gift of God. I thank my Father for both, and pray for all to see my Spirit first!

But let it be the inward adorning and beauty of the hidden person of the heart, with the incorruptible and unfading charm of a gentle and peaceful spirit, which (is not anxious or wrought up, but) is very precious in the sight of God.

1 Peter 3:4

Your outer appearance or circumstances should not define who you are. Your body is merely a suit you put on daily to live in this world. God created us Spirit first, then soul, and lastly body (read first three chapters of Genesis). You live in a world that is blinded by what they can see, not knowing that the best is in the unseen. Don't be concerned with what the world 'thinks' about you; focus on what God 'knows' about you. You may just realize you're awesome after all!

February 4, 2002 Monday Morning

Dear God,

I pray and ask for these specific prayers to be answered:

-Stability at a company or direction by February 15.
Date answered: February 7 at Mercedes (Thank You God!)

-To have the financials to secure different living arrangements by February 15.
Date answered: February 20 Avalon @ Westgrove (Thank You!)

-To have light in a God fearing companion. Taking the same walk with me. In Your time with this one God.
Date Answered: February KG revealed his new faith in God, his tithing, and his spiritual readings. (Thank You, God, please bless our friendship. Please, may it be for a lifetime.)

-Send opportunity and insight on selling real estate.
Date answered: Not yet, receiving a lot of wisdom on it currently. I believe God wants me to buy soon, not sell.

-Start dance classes.
Date answered: March 24 Modern Dance Classes.

-An amazing breakthrough with my acting career.
Date answered: Not God's will for me at this time.

Keep on asking and it will be given you; keep on seeking and you will find; keep on knocking (reverently) and (the door) will be opened to you. — For everyone who keeps on asking receives; and he who keeps on seeking finds; and to him who keeps on knocking, (the door) will be opened.

Matthew 7:7-8

❧ It is true God knows exactly what we need and desire. It's up to us to release our request to Him for movement. God desires to give us what we need but He has blessed us with "free will" to choose His provision when we make our request. Speak it, to receive it. Just a little reminder, beware of what you ask for you just might get it!

Febraury 4, 2002   6:55 p.m.

God forgive me. I felt the need to list my prayers specifically. I truly want Your will for me not my own. I know You will fill my heart's desires, because You put the desires there. I will continue to pray for Your will and be happy.

I pray and ask for Your will God, I invite you. Please work in and through me. Tracy.

February 5, 2002   Tuesday   10:25 p.m.

Dear God,

Thank You for this day of amazing awareness and realization to why particular changes are happening in my life.

Today is my mom's birthday. Thank You for making it possible for me to buy her flowers and take her to dinner. She really appreciated it. I love when I can make someone's day brighter. Thanks to You!

I woke up this morning praying for Your will to be done in my day. I decided to just let You guide me; something I should do always, but today I did and WOW what a day! I will journal the occurrences of this blessed day in the morning. I'm tired.

Now the Lord is the Spirit, and where the Spirit of the Lord is, there is liberty (emancipation from bondage, freedom). And all of us, as with unveiled face, (because we) continued to behold (in the Word of God) as in a mirror the glory of the Lord, are constantly being transfigured (changed) into His very own image in ever increasing splendor and from one degree of glory to another; (for this comes) from the Lord (Who is) the Spirit.

2 Corinthians 3:17-18 AMP

🍃 Change is good, without it growth would be at a stand still. Once you completely surrender and let God perform His goodness in your life you will be set free from experiencing the same ole', same ole' and His nature will show through you. The negativity will slowly decay being replaced with the newness of life and the peace that comes with it. The seed of God in you brings this change forth as you feed it His Word.

February 6, 2002   Wednesday   6:46 a.m.

As I followed Your guide through my conscience awareness yesterday, I was led to go to the real estate office today for due diligence on selling and also was prompted to pursue a long-time desire to fill out an application at a Mercedes-Benz dealership.

I went to the real estate office, and no one was there to help me so I ended up at my Land Rover dealer, because I had time to spare. While I was waiting on a general service visit, I was empowered to ask a salesperson, "Other than the downtown Loeber Mercedes is there another location in the area?" Fortunately, there was one within a few miles, so I decided to just pop in. I know this was Your will showing forth God, because my plans were real estate. It was obvious you wanted me to go to Mercedes.

I stopped in or should I say You sent me in to meet with this surprisingly wonderful sales manager who really didn't have the time, but sat down with me anyway. After I finished filling out my application. For several hours, this kind man spoke with me, educated me, and lifted my spirit about the car business. Man, I was truly there for a reason. This was Your plan God. I was told that only on rare occasions will they consider hiring someone with no car sales experience, but he would consider me. I showed confidence and strength through You God, and my eyes were filled with sincerity. Thank You God. Once again I know this was Your doing.

Who would of figured I'd end up being there for several hours with a manager that was initially, "too busy." A walk-in turned into an afternoon spent researching one of the many desires in my heart. I also had, earlier that day, asked for Your will to be done God.

By the way, this sales manager ran the sister BMW store. The following day (which is today) he insisted on securing an appointment for me with the manager of the original Mercedes dealership I'd stopped in yesterday. Bless this appointment God, may Your hand be with me. Thank You.

After my appointment was over, the blessed sales manager was so impressed with me that he wanted me to meet with his BMW group, just in case. He says he will or may have an opening (although he didn't have one at first). Although he possibly wanted to hire me, he wanted me to follow my true desire and focus on Mercedes-Benz.

With Your strength God, and through prayer, I can conquer this challenge and bring smiles to everyone (customers, the company and myself).

Also, God this day was filled with people at the dealership and the remainder of my day with friends and family who praised Your name! It felt good to be around those with Your glory in common. Bring me more of these days and the strength to handle adversity.

Thank You my Father.

<u>February 6, 2002</u>   <u>Evening</u>

Dear God,

I interviewed today per Your will with Mercedes-Benz. It was a challenge (male dominated industry), but with Your strength I will be top-salesperson in the years to come. I'll say end of 2002 or 2003. Should You bless me with this position. Please bless me with a great memory and wisdom necessary for conquering these goals. May Your hand be with me on my entire journey.

I will make You proud, I will make others happy and I will be prosperous.

By the way, I have not shared this with anyone. I will not until You bless me with it.

Blessed be thou of the Lord, my daughter… — And now, my daughter, fear not; I will do to thee all that thou requirest: for all the city of my people doth know that thou art a virtuous woman (worthy, brave, and capable).

Ruth 3:10-11 AMP

❧ I had to realize that what God has for me, no one can take away. Only I can choose not to receive it by my choices when it's presented to me. The world had me thinking I could not share what was going on in my life until it happened, for fear of what others would think if it didn't. The world is a big liar! You need to share and speak the unseen to have it brought forth wisely.

February 7, 2002   Thursday   Evening

Dear God,

Thank You for teaching me and blessing me with the knowledge to know You should keep your heart's true desires sacred. Only You should know of them.

I would like to share how You bless me when it happens, but in such a way to acknowledge Your goodness. I pray for Your strength, and Your wisdom daily to be all that I can be. Thank You for awareness. I have claimed the Mercedes' position as my prosperous career opportunity that I prayed for only a month ago. This position will be blessed and anointed by You. I will share my happiness with those who can understand and appreciate Your goodness, not with those who have deaf ears. I know this challenge will bring on many more, and I may be too weak to handle them, but I will continually lay those challenges on Your shoulders for guidance, strength, support and knowledge.

I look forward to making people smile. I look forward to making myself smile. I look forward to letting You use me for great works.

Trust (lean on, rely on, and be confident) in the Lord and do good; so shall you dwell in the land and feed surely on His faithfulness, and truly you shall be fed. Delight yourself also in the Lord, and He will give you the desires and secret petitions of your heart. Commit your way to the Lord (roll and repose each care of your load on Him); trust (lean on, rely on, and be confident) also in Him and He will bring it to pass.
Psalms 37:3-5 AMP

❧ God wants to be our best friend as we trust and rely on Him to bring our hearts desires into visibility. If it's "His will" that you pray for it will surely be seen, it will come to pass. (In His time.)

Career Blessing

Dear God,

Today You have blessed me with my next challenge; only with You shall I succeed. Thank You for fulfilling me my heart's desire to sell Mercedes-Benz's. I will be the best! I will sell an amazing amount of cars. I will make people happy. I will put my all into it. I will use all my advantages (inner and outer beauty, being the only woman at the dealership, being African-American) to work for me. I will know daily, it is You who is strengthening me. Bless me with the product knowledge necessary to be the best I can be. Sure, at first this position will not bring the finances I need (because of straight commission), but I know as I make my way through learning and building, You will supply my needs and guide me toward goodness.

I'm off to the Auto Show with my best friend, Sharon to learn and become aware of what I will be selling. Please keep Your hand with me, so that

I may learn and retain knowledge today. Thank You God!

This book of the Law shall not depart out of your mouth, but you shall metitate on it day and night, that you may observe and do according to all that is written in it. For then you shall make your way prosperous, and then you shall deal wisely and have good success.

Joshua 1:8 AMP

You must meet new challenges head-on knowing that God has your back! Think positive and know that **if** God places you He will never give you more than you can handle. The prerequisite to true success is meditating on God's word day and night. Most importantly, it's **doing** what is written in it!

February 10, 2002   Sunday   Morning

*"At last I have come to know God, all roads will be made smooth"
(From Daily Meditations for Woman)*

Dear God,

Thank You for Your goodness. Thank You for Your love.

God, thank You for my answered prayer.

I continue to pray the prayer of Jabez, believing that all I desire will come and you will give me no more than I can handle as I keep You first in my life.

I will continue this prayer. You have blessed me with a challenging career.

I pray to have an enlarged territory. I pray to sell two cars before the end of February, to help with my finances.

I pray to receive an advance or guarantee from Mercedes to get me started, since I'm on straight commission.

I thank You for the knowing of Your shield around me. For the two days of confidence in helping me to secure this position. You were there. At the very beginning, You brought/presented Steven, a positive individual (the light) to me. Then I met with a challenging individual who displayed negativity, and then after we handled the challenge together, God,

You sent me more positive light through the owner of the dealership eventually giving me victory. The job is mine!

Thank You for being there. I look forward to the next chapter of my life You are blessing me with. I know You will never leave me. I promise I will never leave You. I'm so ready for Your infinite blessings, the unseen; and so done with what I thought were blessings in this world! "Be gone satan, I have a protective shield, God's love."

February 10, 2002   1:30 p.m. after church

Today, a pastor who goes to my gym invited me to a church service. Thank You for him and bless the congregation. Jesus' name is powerful! God thank You for Your Son.

Thank You for the Holy Spirit. All I have to do is love and praise you. That's all I have to do.

God made me aware of the POWER in the Name of Jesus on this day. I still had more to learn. It goes to show you that a message can be anywhere. You have to go where the Holy Spirit guides you. Today I had not attended my church home.

February 11, 2002   Monday   Evening

God thank You for my true friend, Sharon

I received a wonderful message from her today. I really prayed and thanked You for my friendship and my success at Mercedes.

Dear God I pray for her:

Oh God bless Sharon, bless her indeed; enlarge her territory (career & family). Oh, that Your hand be with her and keep evil from her.

Wow, she is truly a blessing. I am honored and truly blessed to have her as a life-long friend. She has always showed and amplified her best interests towards me. She knows my ups and my downs. She knows when I was in darkness, and she knows when I received light. I trust her, respect her, and love her unconditionally. Her kindness continually uplifts me. Thank You God for having us be there for one another. She is truly a spiritual sister who continues to help keep me focused on You!

P.S. God, I pray that Sharon believes in herself just as much as she believes in others. There is nothing she can't do. We are all great expressions. We all possess strength, passion, and desires that we can have when we acknowledge who we are. The Holy Spirit is the one within us making it possible for us to tackle and apprehend our hearts desires and dreams.

I have no doubt that it is Christ who strengthens me. I have no doubts about myself. I will have my hearts desires. I will build relationships that make people smile and make them feel love at Mercedes and where ever I go.

Thank You God for my awareness, and for my new beginning. At 33 years of age I finally know what makes my world, You!

Oh, what a great discovery! You have always been here!

Constantly praising God and being in favor and goodwill with all the people; and the Lord kept adding (to their number) daily those who were being saved (from spiritual death).

Acts 2:47 AMP

🍃 It is vital that as you began to grow spiritually that you surround yourself with individuals that can enhance your walk and not hinder it. Girlfriends that are in love with Jesus are perfectly wrapped gifts from God! Aren't you ready to have conversations that don't just center around the men in your life?

<u>February 12, 2002</u>   <u>Tuesday</u>   <u>Morning</u>

First, thank You God for letting me wake-up and thank You for a great knowledge-filled first day at Mercedes.

I woke up mid-morning and had a vision that Mark was in the midst of something with the Feds. I still don't know what Mark really does for a living. God, let him share things with me today. Bring this mystery to light about this man I seem to love, so that I may pray for him and for whatever he needs to do to get out. I know he wants to live right. He just thinks he has to come to You guilt-free and sin-free, though I continue to share with him that You want us just the way we are.

Over the past few nights, You woke me with visions, powerful visions for my future. I know that if I can envision myself doing what my heart desires, I can see it manifest in this world with the help of the Holy Spirit, sent by Jesus. You must first be able to see it.

God, I live for and want the Holy Spirit to work through me and guide me. Oh Lord, please use me.

Your dream and the visions in your head upon your bed are these: As for you, O king, as you were lying upon your bed thoughts came into your mind about what should come to pass hereafter, and He Who reveals secrets was making known to you what shall come to pass.

Daniel 2:28b-29 AMP

❧ You can't pick and chose your dreams like I was doing in and at this point. Accepting the dream regarding my future but not allowing myself to accept the vision about Mark being in trouble, because I didn't want him to be involved in wrong doings.

❧ God will bring you visions and dreams no matter where you are or what time it is. You need to recognize the vision, the message being sent, whether it is a dream, an instinct or written sign. See it, believe it, and it will manifest.

February 15, 2002   Friday   Morning

My time has come. I can mold my future. I will take each day, each experience, and let it draw to me the next important steps.

Dear God,

Oh, how I feel Your presence. I know I can do anything with the Holy Spirit in me! I now realize that the past four months were a time for me to be in prayer. I have become so close to You God. I feel so protected. Every time adversity is presented, the Holy Spirit stirs up something positive in me or sends me some "positivity." I feel so special, so loved. I feel that everyone around me knows my love for You. Keep me with You. Use me. For I never want to go back to a life that does not involve realizing Your perfect love.

I must say You are truly keeping evil from me. Thank You God.

And this I speak for your own profit; not that I may cast a snare upon you, but for that which is comely, and that ye may attend upon the Lord without distraction.

I Corinthians 7:35

God was removing friends and situations out of my life, so that I would keep my focus on Him and not be distracted. You may not see at the exact moment when a change occurs in your life that you feel isn't for the better, but God has a way of reaching you even when you try and distract yourself. It becomes your responsibility to not allow the same circumstance or relationships to interfere down the path. Satan will place the same distraction in front of you; you must say you no longer will accept this type of person or circumstance in your life.

February 15, 2002   Friday   Evening

Dear God,

Thank You for sending true believers to me at Mercedes, so I may know who You have around to protect me, to teach me, and to show me love. Bless Tony and Joseph, both being men of God, who have the Holy Spirit truly within them. Thank You for the kind angels I continue to run across. It's very peaceful to know I am protected. Please bless Luis a porter here at Mercedes and his kindness. I pray to sell cars tomorrow, my first real day on the sales floor. I am asking to sell some cars Lord.

I have been faced with the reality that I have to move March 1. I have no savings. I don't know what my mom is going to do, because she's currently living with me. I don't get paid at work until I sell some cars, my car note is due, my finances ... I will stop complaining and start praying.

God thank you for placing me in a commissioned career because I know in time that it will be "very" prosperous. God please guide my next steps in finding the finances to move, where to move, and bless my mother with the same. If it is meant for me to ask my friends, please open the door for me.

God please let me be accepted at a real estate property regardless of past credit history; please open the door for my mom and myself. Talk to me in my dreams okay God? Give me answers to my living situation; send opportunity my way before the end of the month. Bless Richard (my present landlord).

God, I am asking and praying for a miracle. I need strength, for I know I'm under attack because of my faith in the unseen. I know my prayers will be answered.

Thank You Jesus, Thank You God!

Oh God bless me, bless me indeed. Enlarge my territory God. Oh that Your hand be with me. Keep me from evil so that I may not cause or feel pain.

For you have need of steadfast patience and endurance, so that you may perform and fully accomplish the will of God, and thus receive and carry away (and enjoy to the full) what is promised.
Hebrews 10:36 AMP

❧ Remember you will feel as though you are under attack, what your self wills to happen may not if it is not in line with God's will. You must take this as a sign that you are stepping closer to God and your will is becoming more evident when it is not God's purpose for you.

February 16, 2002   Saturday   Evening

God thank You for this day! Thank You for the opportunity to minister to someone in need, to be able to uplift and edify him or her with Your truth. Please bless Tracee, a friend and former coworker. She just called out of the blue. She said that she just needed someone to talk to, some positive words. You used me God, thank You. It felt so good to hear her say to me, Tracy thank you for being there for me. You are such a beautiful person inside and out. I'm glad something made me dial your number." I know it was You God. This young lady rarely calls. Please continue to use me. It's wonderful when people have an ear to listen.

Bless a new car customer I helped today and enlarge my business relationship with him.

I love You ... I love You. Continue to keep evil from me. Thank You.

Are not the angels all ministering spirits (servants) sent out in the service (of God for the assistance) of those who are to inherit salvation?   Hebrews 1:14 AMP

As a child of God having a sincere heart for others your Heavenly Father will direct those, in need of upifting, to you. A few good words can make someone's day. A few good words of the Truth that is!

SELF

For I know nothing good dwells within me, that is, in my flesh. I can will what is right, but I cannot perform it. (I have the intention and urge to do what is right, but no power to carry it out).

But I discern in my bodily members (in the sensitive appetites and wills of the flesh) a different law (rule of action) at war against the law of my mind (my reason) and making me a prisoner to the law of sin that dwells in my bodily organs (in the sensitive appetites and wills of the flesh)

O unhappy and pitable and wretched man that I am! Who will release and deliver me from (the shackles of) this body of death?

O thank God! (He will) through Jesus Christ (the Anointed One) our Lord! So then indeed I, of myself with the mind and heart, serve the Law of God, but with the flesh the law of sin.

Romans 7:18, 23-25 AMP

✎ **SELF PLEASER:** It's all about Me, Myself and I; Soul, Body, and Spirit (in order of importance); "Born Again" repenting and asking for change with a sincere heart; baptism into the death and resurrection of Jesus (die to guilt and sin of the past); reality and power of God's Word is understandable as I study for myself; my permissible will instead of God's perfect will; presence of Christ in me (the anointing); consecration begins (getting rid of the old baggage in the soul and replacing it with fruits of God's character); Unsanctified Bride of Christ (Heart filled with past sin-lying, anger, jealousy, vain, deceit, unloving, depression, loneliness, hate, unforgiving); desire to know the real me (God's definition);

Immature in the Spirit; In and out of God's presence; realization of freedom from sin/bondage; conviction with no condemnation; partial obedience; thank God for all He is doing for me (selfish); praise more than worship to God; satisfaction in "self"; **yet another Spiritual level to go.**

February 18, 2002   Monday   Evening

Dear God,

Thank You for baptizing my Holy Spirit yesterday at Living Word Christian Center here in Chicago, where Bill Winston is the anointed Pastor. I thank You for the message from my coworker Joseph, to be baptized and cleansed of all my past sins (behavior and thoughts) and make me anew. Although I felt over the past several months that my mind was being renewed, I now have a new understanding. The enemy was using my past sins (debt, confusion, fornication, doubt, and so on) to keep me in bondage.

Wisdom is the principal thing; therefore get wisdom: and with all thy getting get understanding.

Proverbs 4:7

Now, I've come from being a loss believer. "Born Again" in the Name of Jesus Christ I have a real opportunity to be a new individual. This opportunity by far beats the career opportunity at Mercedes You blessed me with. Spiritual awareness and knowledge will get me all that is promised; peace, prosperity, goodness, debt-free, love and no evil will prevail even if it presents itself.

I rebuke the things of satan in the Name of Jesus Christ!!

Thank You dear God, for the ability to communicate with You through speaking in tongues. I know You understand and hear me. Amen.

Bless mother and me, bless us indeed. Enlarge our territories. Oh that Your hand be with us, and keep evil from us. Amen.

Then Peter said unto them, repent, and be baptized every one of you in the name of Jesus Christ for the remission of sins, and ye shall receive the gift of the Holy Ghost.

Acts 2:38

❧ Once you have repented for your sins and received Jesus as Lord, only at that time do you have a personal relationship with God, and his Holy Spirit lives in you. You are "Born Again". We are all born as sinners, and we need to repent to come into a true relationship with God. Your goodness can't do it, but your humbleness can. There is yet another gift that God has made available to those who choose to believe; the power of the Holy Ghost. This power ignites your Holy Spirit with spiritual gifts that prepare you for the spiritual warfare you have been living in, without knowing it. Once again you war against spiritual wickedness, not flesh (people). You need power to tell the satan to go!

You need power to discern between good and bad! You need power to communicate (speak) with God from your spirit, not your flesh! You need power to hold on to the anointing (the Christ in you)! You need power to receive and understand the mysteries (revelations) found in God's Word (the Bible)! You need power to do signs and miracles! Jesus was our example. It was not until He was baptized (fully submerged in water) that he started doing miracles. It is the Word that brings this power. This is an ultimate desire of the Holy Spirit to be activated, to be plugged into God's miracle working POWER!

February 20, 2002　　　Wednesday　　　1:30 p.m.

Dear God,

I just received a call from MGM studios to play a feature spot with no lines in a movie with Cedric the Entertainer (close friend). This was the film that was being produced by George Tillman. It will shoot all day tomorrow during my work hours at Mercedes. Should I take the opportunity to work or network my Mercedes business?

Tracy L. Moss

February 20, 2002   5:30 p.m.

Thank You God for my answer. My manager thought it would be a great idea to go. I thought he would not approve of me being out the entire day, but, it is through You that opportunity happens. Please be with me all day tomorrow. I praise and glorify You!!!

✍ I'm still living of the self, no longer of the world but still of my "self" wanting to fill my own needs. You may take small steps back, it is not an overnight process. You have spent years living of the world and of the self; it may take time to learn to live of the Spirit. Do not punish yourself, just be aware and correct your footing by calling on the help of the Holy Spirit.

Febraury 20, 2002   Evening

Dear God,

Thank You for sending assistance with my move. My savings are depleted and my move could not be possible without faith in You and the miracles You send my way. A few of my friends offered to pay for a moving service, and another has decided to send me money via mail while he's on the road traveling with his team. I never asked; I know this is all You, God.

Bless them all and thank You.

God, I have looked at a total of three apartments. I have prayed that my past not affect the outcome of me receiving the place of Your will. But, I know that with Your will, You will place me at the apartment or home my heart desires. I believe in You! I love You.

And God is able to make all grace abound toward you; that ye, always having all sufficiency in all things may abound to every good work.

II Corinthians 9:8

God made grace abound toward the hearts of my friends, to help me though I did not ask them. When you sincerely believe God will supply your every need, God will show up and show out.

February 21, 2002   Thursday   Morning

Good morning God,

Dear Father I have eight days left to secure another place to stay. I have no income yet, but I know through Your grace that a door is going to open,

118

finances will come soon to support my move. No commission yet at Mercedes, because I'm still learning the product. May Your will be done, Lord.

Mark has just asked me to be his roommate. Give me clarity, direction, and Your will in this. I have not answered his question. Please guide me, and tell me how to answer and what to do. Thank You God.

Also, I was called last night by the film's casting director and told, "Usually this doesn't happen, but we've been told you don't have to be here all day. We will call you when your scene is coming." (Normally all actors have to be around all day.) Thank you God, for Your anointing. Now I can be at work part of the day.

🌿 I have been placed where my Father God would like for me to be at this moment. The enemy continues to use other career opportunities and men as distractions. Stay focused on your walk with the Lord.

February 21, 2002   2:30 p.m.

Dear God,

I praise and glorify Your name. I was just told by an apartment complex, I truly desire to move in to, that my credit was approved and I could move in March 1st! I did not let doubt come. Whenever I felt it, I'd rebuke satan in the Name of Jesus Christ. Before I renewed my mind I know I would have talked that apartment away from me, worried about my past credit. Heck, I haven't worked for nearly five months and have been blessed with an awesome place to live with a workout facility and a swimming pool on site! When you believe and don't let anything of satan creep into your life, God will open doors you never imagined – big or small.

Hallelujah, all praise to God!

Blessings acknowledged:

± New job with a company that never hires without experience; this was a first time for them.
± Secured a luxury apartment home just in time, with a move-in date of March 1.

Glory to God!!! Thank You Jesus!!!
Doubt is of satan, not of God.

February 23, 2002   Saturday   7:15 a.m.

Dear God,

I have repented yesterday's sins (looseness to please my relationship). Please be new in me. Please forgive me. Thank You.

Today started with a challenge and his name is Mark. Our relationship is confusing; it's like dating Dr. Jekyll and Mr. Hyde at times. One moment he's supporting my walk and next, he doesn't want to hear anything about You, God. I left his home today feeling like I've lost my integrity because I lay with him, but expected him to respect my need to not be intimate.

❧ Temptation, trying to please others by rejecting your true nature will cause you to step off your path. Turn to God for strength; ask for His help to show you what He wants.

I rebuke the things of evil, I pray, "Oh God bless me, bless me indeed. Enlarge my territory. Oh, that Your hand be with me and to keep evil from me that I seem to not be able to stay away from." Thank You God.

Thank You God for this day. Thank You for waking me this morning. Thank You for choices and Love.

Thank You for the apparent answer regarding moving in with Mark, no! There is nothing in the Bible that shows it's okay to live with a man. This choice will lead to even more fornication. It's not right!

... The seed is the word of God.

Luke 8:11

🌿 By reading the Word of God, the Bible, I was able to get the answer to my question concerning rooming with my companion at that time. I didn't read anything about rooming with a companion, so I knew it was not of God. All my choices are starting to be geared toward God's direction, not my own. I also realized that God is not a God of confusion. This was apparently not a relationship from Him.

February 23, 2002   7:02 p.m.

Dear God,

Oh, blessed be the Lord. I said through Your grace I would make a choice to turn my day to fruits of You, to keep my mind on those things that are good. Thank You, God for blessing me with my 1st car sale at Mercedes. Bless Dan and Sharon and their son. Thank You for them. Thank You for their smiles.

Being filled with the fruits of righteousness, which are by Jesus Christ, unto the glory and praise of God.

Philippians 1:11

⚜ No matter how my day started, it will end great because I chose to have an awesome day. It was my choice. Wake each morning envisioning the day you will experience. Pray to God aloud thanking Him in advance for the patience, love, excitement, and qualities you want brought to fruition.

<u>February 24, 2002</u>   Sunday   Evening

Dear God,

Thank You for a blessed day. Thank you for the confidence and courage to recite poetry during our Sunday service at Unity of Oak Park.

God, I am now receiving career opportunities. Please make me realize that the career I'm in right now is the one You want me in. While applying for this job at Mercedes, I continued to pray for Your will. Is this Your will? Why am I receiving all of these other employment offers now? Why didn't I receive them when I was out of work for months? Is it satan trying to keep me away from Your perfect plan? I actually have to say I love what I'm doing. I sold my first car through Your grace. I know this position is hard, dedicated work compared to the offers of salaried positions, but I know with Your strength and light we can make this position number one.

❧ Yes that was satan, he loves to get you to give up on a blessing from God just before you reach the success God has for you. Satan loves for you to give up in the middle, and God loves for you to endure until the end for victory. You can't see it, but with faith you know it's there.

God, I have to move in one week, You have blessed me with a check from KG (bless him) of $1000. I still need at least $2000 more. My car note is past due. God I know You continue to supply my needs and I thank You. Please help me achieve a debt-free life. Oh, how my heart would feel so much better. I don't know what to do about my finances God.

My people are destroyed for lack of knowledge: because thou hast rejected knowledge.

Hosea 4:6a

Can You please bless me with some car sales, and a miracle check. Please I pray and ask for this. Thank You. Now I must believe!

Please God let me know that I am living Your will right now. Please show me more of Your light. The enemy is trying to bring doubt in my life. I rebuke the enemy in the name of Jesus!

This evening I saw an inspiring documentary on Rosa Parks; I actually look like a younger version of her. She had and made all the right choices and received more!

I can and will become the first woman at Mercedes to achieve top sales, and who knows, maybe I'll eventually be hired by Mercedes-Benz, USA.

🌿 What should have been said at the end of this statement is "God, if this is Your perfect will, I will eventually be hired with Mercedes-Benz USA." God may have something in His kingdom (here on the earth) for me to do full-time--sharing the good news. He may not have me at a corporation for long, promotion comes from God not man!

February 26, 2002　　　Tuesday　　　Evening

Dear God,

Thank You for peace, for surrounding me with people of You, and for Your Word. For I know if I continue to let You guide me in making the right choices, the true desires of my heart will shine and manifest.

God bless Tony and his wife of 25 years. Also, bless Joseph and his wife of 23 years. They are true men of you. I appreciate being around them at Mercedes as I continue to learn and know how good Your grace and anointing is.

Thank You God for enlarging my client base. Today I worked with a lot of people whom You sent to me. It was truly a blessing. I know I will receive their car sales, when they are ready. Thank You for my past experience in customer relations. This personality You have blessed me with stands out above the rest. Thank You.

If then you have been raised with Christ (to a new life, thus sharing His resurrection from the dead), aim at and seek the (rich, eternal treasures) that are above, where Christ is, seated at the right hand of God.

Colossians 3:1 AMP

❦ You sit far above the world once you accept Jesus the Christ in you. This is an example of how I felt and I didn't know this scripture just yet. God's Word does not lie.

Bless my mother, Oh Lord; bless her indeed. Please place her in housing that she can be comfortable in and not lonely. I will always be there for her. Please allow her to utilize this housing organization as a resource to take her to where she would like to be, which is her own house or home in a drug-free area because the last place she lived in since moving to Chicago was not the best area. Allow her to stay in Your Word during this transition. I love You God!

February 27, 2002   Wednesday   7 p.m.

Dear God,

Yesterday was filled with anxieties thinking about the unknown. Father, You know I have a lot of new beginnings happening. First, a full time relationship with You; second, a new sales career; third, a new apartment; fourth, end of a relationship that was not sent by You; and last but not least, my mother venturing back on her own.

So, I prayed a lot yesterday because I felt lonely and a little lost, but You saved me once again with a great reading in the Bible about the faith in the unseen, and gave me phone calls from friends bringing uplifting words. Thank You. I feel the light again, I must say the darkness never last long. My reading confirmed that the unknown is filled with great potential and growth! I must continue to stay on Your path and keep the faith. My Father has plenty in store for me. I welcome it! I love You Dad, God, my Father. My everything!

Now faith is the substance of things hoped for, the evidence of things not seen.

Hebrews 11:1

You see that a man is justified (pronounced righteous before God) through what he does and not alone through faith (through works of obedience as well as by what he believes). — For as the human body apart from the Spirit is lifeless, so faith apart from its works of obedience is also dead.

James 2:24,26 AMP

Even the knowledge that you are walking towards living in the Spirit, of releasing your control and allowing the Spirit to guide you can be fearful. You have always been in control and the sense that you lose control can keep you from God. Fear is satan. God will not let you fall nor lead you into suffering, His path through His Spirit will only lead to peace and a life you should be living. Satan wants you to remain living for self and for the world because he can control you, destroy you; plague you with loss, suffering, disappointment and madness. Once you live in and through the Spirit, satan can no longer reach you. God lifts you out of satan's reach and you become a soul that can reach down and raise other spirits out of satan's hand.

March 1, 2002   Friday   1:20 p.m.

Dear Gracious, All-Knowing, Loving, and Forgiving God,

Let this be a page full of praising and lifting up of Your name. A page filled with praising and thanks for Your son, my Lord and Savoir, Jesus Christ.

Tears of joy come to my eyes when I think of Your goodness. As I think about how You continue to save me by making me aware of my past choices that were not of You. I thank You for my mother's awareness of Your goodness. I thank You for all of the people You continue to place and present in my life. Thank You, because I now know the difference between You and the world. I choose You!!

Thank You for positive thoughts, for smiles, for love, for security, for comfort, for spiritual growth, for financial growth, for family, for friends, for today. I praise and glorify Your name. I love You, God. I love You, Jesus!

For (simply) consider your own call, brethren; not many (of you were considered to be) wise according to human estimates and standards, not many influential and powerful, not many of high and noble birth.   I Corinthians 1:26 AMP

✄ As current situations place you in a position to live by the world's standards you will recognize the blessings you receive are from God and not because of what you have done in trying to please the world. Living up to any standard created by man vs. living in God's likeness is like the difference between life and death.

March 4, 2002   Monday   Morning

Dear God,

Good morning! I love You, I feel You, and I feel the Holy Spirit within me. There is nothing I can't do. Thank You for giving me strength! Thank You for giving my mother strength!

Today's a big day. My move is almost complete (thank You) and my mother is going into her temporary housing tonight or tomorrow. Please God keep Your hand with us both. Allow us to know that we are

*not alone. Give us Your light daily. Allow my moth-
er to journey and take the steps towards all that she
wants. Allow this move to give us strength. May we
both still be there for one another, "Detachment with
Love attached." Bless my only brother, may he
know we are in "Good" hands! Place my mother
where she may find peace and adequate assistance in
her next living arrangement. Bless her with a home.
Thank You God!!*

Bless my family and myself, indeed!!

Come close to God and He will come close to you. (Recognize that you are) sinners, get your soiled hands cleaned; (realize that you have been disloyal) wavering individuals with divided interests, and purify your hearts (of your spiritual adultery).

James 4:8 AMP

❧ You need to realize that living with "detachment with love attached" is accepting that you cannot be responsible for saving the ones you love. Only God can save. You must come to God of your own will not through another's. Love those in your life, pray for them but know it is ultimately their responsibility and choice to have a sincere heart, to change that God may choose them.

<u>March 9, 2002</u>   <u>Saturday</u>   <u>7 p.m.</u>

Dear God,

Thank You for a blessed week. Thank You for a blessed day. I continue to get answers to questions I have yet to ask, when it comes to living right and living for You, God. Thank You.

I know I must study and read the Bible daily, as often as I brush my teeth. Please continue to guide me as I locate a Bible study class.

If I want peace, love, kindness, security, happiness, and all good in my life I must know the Word, Your Word, my Creator's Word, the BIBLE.

I must not let anything or anyone tempt me into disobeying Your Word. I pray for strength; I will surrender all tempting acts. You have been so good to me that I don't want to trade this treatment for the world's disappointments.

I love You, God.

Wisdom is the principal thing; therefore get wisdom: and with all thy getting get understanding.

Proverbs 4:7

My people are destroyed for lack of knowledge: because thou hast rejected knowledge...

Hosea 4:6a

Study to show thyself approved unto God, a workman that needeth not to be ashamed, rightly dividing the word of truth.

2 Timothy 2:15 AMP

❧ God's Word is spiritual food for the new "Born Again" Spirit. The Spirit needs nurturing and feeding exactly like our mortal bodies for growth. Your Spirit is the only "tour guide" to the perfect plan God has already established for your life. For true victory in your Christian walk your Spirit has to get the majority of your attention, then your soul and body. The Holy Spirit will introduce you to all truths and will reveal all the lies you have accepted in the past about yourself. Spiritual knowledge is the key, but what good is it if you receive it and don't live by it.

Hey God,

I love You! Thank you for the joy in my mother's voice; thank you! Thank You for the inner guide encouraging me to buy cards for my brother in prison. I realize and have read in Your scriptures the importance of showing love to those in prison, Jesus would. (Matthew 25:36)

Lord God, Jesus, I woke up this morning feeling lonely. I desire a companion who loves You as I do. I long for and desire to start a family (husband and kids). At one time, I was selfish in my thinking, and I didn't want to ruin my body. But now with this newly found love for You, for myself, and no longer wanting any of the worldly temporary joys; I desire to share and receive love from a man that is of You. I know I can't go wrong if he is of You. I want love, happiness, peace and security. I want a relationship filled with Your love, God. Please bless me with this, bless me indeed. Allow my husband to find me. Thank You.

🌿 I'm changing from gory to glory. I am being renewed daily, and the changes are making me think I am lonely. This is an attempt from satan. As I continue to fall in love with my new found Love that I can't see, Jesus, my lonely pleas for a man will be far and few. I must first be whole inside before God can bless me with the family I desire.

March 12, 2002   Tuesday   Morning

Dear God,

I give You praise. I lift and adore You. I lift and praise Your son's name, Jesus! Thank You, Jesus, for the Holy Spirit within me. Thank You!

I slept on the couch last night; just fell asleep on it, until sometime in the middle of the night when I was awoken by the television. There was some sort of concert on and all I could hear was "Jesus, Jesus" and more songs with Jesus in them! It was amazing because I don't think it was a gospel concert.

I went back to sleep with Jesus all throughout my mind. It was a great sleep. Then I was woken by a call from my mother with cheer and joy in her voice. Thank You God for her found peace.

Boy, when you invite and welcome the Holy Spirit in your life through Jesus, the Son of God, miraculous things happen that you know is all from God.

Also, thank You God, for my first commission check, and thank You for my second check as well. I never knew you could sell one car and make $1,500, but I can and will continue through Jesus Christ who strengthens me!

❧ God will wake you, or bless you in the middle of your day, once you are open to Him. He will send you messages and confirmations. Remain aware as you travel of this world and not for it.

March 13, 2002   Wednesday   8:50 p.m.

Dear God,

Thank You for blessing me with knowing, truth, awareness, Your goodness, Your grace, Your giving and love, lots of love.

Every time I breathe, I feel You. The Holy Spirit is truly within me! Thank You for the love of myself.

True love is when You sigh during the day and feel something special within. That is how and what I feel when I think of Your goodness.

Thank You for Your blessings, thank You.

❧ At this point I am falling in love with what God is doing for me, how He is blessing me, and how He is making me aware of Him. Eventually, I will fall in love with Him, just for Himself and not just for what He can do for me. There will be days when you have let the Spirit guide you completely. It is these days that you must harness and remember for they are a sign that the door is opening between you and God. It takes time but the days when you have completely given yourself over to the Spirit will become more frequent as you grow spiritually.

March 14, 2002   Thursday   10:20 p.m.

Hi there, loving God,

I love You, praise You and adore You. Whenever I need light, You send it to me. Thank You.

I know I continue to pray for financial freedom God, and I do appreciate how You supply for my needs. It's just that I've always seemed to need freedom from debtors, freedom from controlling friends who gave me money. I just need plain old independence. So my focus will not be anywhere but on my true love for You.

Well ... once again, You sent someone with my answer. I know You send answers to our problems always, all the time, but sometimes we don't listen. My answer was to make a goal! I'm in car sales now and must strive with the strength of the Holy Spirit to make specific monthly/yearly goals. To push myself, I must view my goal chart daily. I must continue to educate myself on cars, as I do with the Word. It's the only way to grow. I must educate myself daily in all that I want prosperity in. Thank You, God.

❧ I now have the best teacher ever, the Holy Spirit. Learning could never be easier or more fulfilling! God has left us instructions (a guide to follow) as we experience our lives here on earth. The Bible is your first source, it is the answer to any situation you may be experiencing.

March 16, 2002   Saturday   6:30 p.m.

Dear God,

Thank You for the challenges of today. I had customers with a lot of questions that I just simply could not answer. I know that these challenges appear for my growth. Please God continue to guide me toward spiritual success that will pave the way for all else.

My day at Mercedes was busy; I know You continue to bless me with potential clients and I thank You. I felt the need today for more training. Mercedes sales training! Within hours You blessed me by sending my manager over to offer me award-winning training next week! You heard my cry instantly. Thank You. I pray to God that this training will dramatically assist me in my "on the spot" selling.

God, throughout this training please have Your hands with me. Bless me with the ability to listen, understand, put to action and remember what I am taught. I know I can do nothing without my Holy Spirit, made available by Jesus Christ, guiding me along the way, through Your grace of course. Thank You and I love You, Father.

✿ God knows what we need before we ask, but we must verbally make our request known for the angels to move in making it happen!

March 17, 2002   Sunday   11:30 a.m.

Dear God,

Thank You for Helice and Unity of Oak Park. These are the key points that You made me aware of in her message today:

Lesson was on "Freeing Ourselves From Bondage" Release anything that is unlike light. Anything that doesn't align with God's Word.

Know the truth and practice it. Walk it, not just talk it.

Have a higher level of consciousness for more. Know that better is there for the asking.

A prayerful soul can't be hidden; You shine like a light. Love has a glow that will be recognized. God is Love.

People will come to you to know what lets your light shine, at this time you begin to lift others.

Every destructive thought is limiting and harmful to your growth.

Bringing up old unconscious thoughts will not help you grow, choose to release the past and let go. Go to a higher level of consciousness. Get "Born Again." Give up the lesser for the greater. Give up your ways, for God's ways. Leading to life, instead of death.

Power center is our throat and words speak truth. You can speak blessings or curses into your life.

I prayed for the opportunity to minister today, the opportunity to share Your Word and inspire another.

You sent me: Darrell (my mom's companion), Raymond (a friend from my hometown), my grandma, and Tracee (friend and sister in Christ). After speaking with them all individually, Your Word was heard and felt. Bless them all. May they see Your light continually.

And it shall come to pass in that day, that his burden shall be taken away from off thy shoulder, and his yoke from off thy neck, and the yoke shall be destroyed because of the anointing.

Isaiah 10:27

 We can't free ourselves from bondage. The anointing of God (his presence) is the only way to be set free.

March 18, 2002 Monday 9:50 p.m.

Thank You God for miracles! Thank You for the personality within me that wins smiles and sincerity. Thank You God for my overall health. Thank You God for the gift of beauty, inside and out, that attracts all types of people. Thank You.

God, I realized that when I let the day flow and not pressure or push anything, You are pleased. This is because the Holy Spirit is working through me. How can I go wrong?

Thank You for my continued financial flow, which is taking care of my needs at this moment.

Testimony

Saturday I was working on a "hot" prospect (someone ready to buy a car). He had a few more questions before finalizing the deal, and this slowed up the process. During this time my blessed brother Tony sold the same car while I was attempting to answer my customers questions. (This can happen occasionally in the car business.) I lost the sale, but I didn't let it depress me. I continued my day blessed by You, with peace and contentment. I just went with the flow and was happy that Tony got the sale. By remaining humble and accepting of what is God, You blessed me with the opportunity to help one of his customers later that day when he had two customers simultaneously. Not only was I able to work with him and learn, Tony returned the favor by offering to *split this sale half and half. How ironic is it that the commission for this deal is going to be exactly the amount I would have received in the first missed sale earlier. God you are so good! Thank You, God.*

❧ Just by being happy and appreciative with what is, the door can be opened for more blessings to flow our way!

March 19, 2002   Tuesday   Morning

Good morning God,

I just wanted to thank You for this day, thank You for waking me. I appreciate You and need You.

I also wanted to make a note about how if you want to change, you can in a blink of an eye. When you are in the Word daily (the Bible) and keeping faith, then God has more for you that you just can't see yet, change is much easier than I assumed!

Here are the changes I have made in the three months under God's Holy Spirit's guidance. (All changes that had good results).

± Choosing to make God my number one priority Listen to all. I am now slow to speak. I am learning a lot daily.
± Becoming satisfied being single.
± Dedication to prayer daily. I ask for God's blessings everyday. I know I am receiving them every time, whether big or small. I must stay obedient.
± My dress code, leaning towards the more conservative look when at the office.
± More time spent alone.
± Patience, being anxious for nothing.
± Trusting in the Lord to supply my every need, not men or people around me.

Growth is the result of change. Maturity brings on this change. I realized I had to be "tired" to desire this necessary change.

March 19, 2002   Evening

Thank You, God for ideas; for many great inspirations to do things that lead to prosperity.

Only several days ago, You gave me the idea to call Krista at Bell Auto Leasing where my vehicle is being leased, and see if we could do business with any clients who may not be able to get financing here at Mercedes. Through referrals I would receive an extra $150, and she would send me customers also! Thank You God for the knowing that I must manifest ideas that are given to us by You.

Bless Krista and my business relationship. God, may we help one another's continued success.

❧ We must put inspiring thoughts or ideas to action in order to be even more blessed/prosperous. God is only of good, trust in that, believe in that, and miracles will happen!

March 20, 2002   Wednesday   9:50 p.m.

Dear God,

I have realized that there is NO greater challenge than living right, being obedient in Your eyes. It is the most challenging job, situation, career, whatever, *a person could ever have. But, the rewards through-out this walk are great and not to be compared. These rewards are peace, newness of life, going in the right direction, and a soul that is being renewed with Love. If I hang in there, God, You will be so proud of me, and You will continue to be in me.*

No worldly challenge can compare to this. True strength shines here!

Jesus answered, If a person (really) loves Me, he will keep My Word (obey my teaching): and My Father will love him, and we will come to him and make Our home (abode, special dwelling place) with him.

John 14:23

🌿 I've had many partners in business, but only true partnership is with the Holy Spirit. He will keep you in the presence of the Lord. As you call on the help God has sent your challenges will not overcome you they will be met with the attitude of knowing that there is already victory! Obey the promptings of the Holy Spirit, He has come to make obedience natural without your frivolous works and good intentions that don't impress God anyway! Obedience is the key!

<u>March 22, 2002</u>   <u>Friday</u>   <u>8:40 p.m.</u>

Dear God,

Thank You for sending me to training on "Basic Car Sales" with Lenny, a great motivator at Mercedes. He persuaded me to read a book called, <u>Think and Grow Rich</u> by Napoleon Hill. As a matter of fact, I just so happen to have this book on my bookshelf from years ago. I don't know where it came from, but I now know why I never got rid of it. All things come together with patience, in Your time.

It turns out that this book, along with my number one reading, The Bible, are the keys to all the successes stirring in my life.

I feel really blessed. There are true qualities I've already been blessed with. My mentor's only had to show and tell me which ones are needed for success. God, You truly have me on the right path, You are preparing me for my good, for my success, for the prosperous life already prepared by You.

Now I see how you can choose to live out your true destiny, the one that God has for you. I just needed the faith and to picture success in all my heart's desires, after I made God first in my life, they are slowly coming to light. You take the challenges that come with it, learn from them, analyze them, and grow from the attempts that are there to defeat you.

This did not dawn on me until my later years. I have always moved from job to job, sales to acting to sales, to events, to finance and now to sales again. Even this Mercedes sales' field is something I've had ideas about many years ago. I'll stick to acquiring top salesperson, as I know that I am no longer a wanderer as I have been in my many careers. I will be dedicated and learn stability until the Lord says differently. It is important for you to become a well-planted seed, bearing my fruit in whatever field or calling you choose. Work is love manifested

I will continue to know that God blesses me daily to overcome and grow from any possible obstacles. It is only fear jumping in my path! Evil tries to make you give up before you reach success. Think success; think true manifestation, true determination, true faith, and only good fortune will be your inheritance.

Now faith is the substance of things hoped for, the evidence of things not seen.

Hebrews 11:1

🌿 Your spiritual turning point is literally moments away when you feel like giving up. Don't go by your feelings. Once you have received the Spirit of the Lord you have to trust in the unseen and know your breakthrough is approaching. You must not let the enemy steal your dreams, by giving up on what you can't see just yet.

March 23, 2002   Sunday   8:50 a.m.

Dear God,

I am the righteous! Sin was created by the devil and the world to take away my trust in being righteous. When I received Jesus Christ as my Lord and Savior, I inherited all rights to happiness.

Thank You my precious Father for I now realize to live daily for You and let Your will control my life. You send people to bless me, saved or not. Tony, a mighty man of God who shares the gospel (the good news of

Jesus) daily with me, notified me that upon his departure from Mercedes, he wants to turn his clients over to me. He's trying to figure out the right way to do it. Thank You God for this blessing, should You make it possible.

Also, as Your child God, people offer me assistance in attaining success at Mercedes. At one point and time I would have said it's because of my beauty. That's how I used to get what I wanted while living "in the world," but today while living in the world but not being "of the world" I know it's just the glow of light I have inside. It's you God sending my daily blessings from and through others. Thank You God!

Neither is there salvation in any other: for there is none other name under heaven given among men, whereby we must be saved.

Acts 4:12

❧ As "Born Again" believers, you must know you are in right standing with God through Jesus' works on the cross, and not of your daily works in the flesh. The name Jesus declares the guilty "not guilty." There is no other name whereby we can be saved.

March 25, 2002   Monday   Evening

Dear God,

Forgive me for making arrangements to pay my debts and not being able to follow through. Please assist me, give me strength as I continue to pray for financial freedom. God I pray to owe no debt. I will organize my debt again and pray on each for Your blessing of freedom from them.

I have and am still learning the difference between a want and a need. I am ready God for more financial blessings. I promise you I can handle it. First to pay my tithes before my bills, then whatever else You would like me to do with the remainder. I will consult You every time for Your guidance God.

Thank You for lessons learned. I love You!!

❧ Money management can be a generational curse. As God's children we are made into great stewards over the wealth that He blesses us with. We must become a new generation that will break the curses of the past by knowing who we are in Christ. This bondage can only be removed through the anointing of God.

March 27, 2002   Wednesday   7:15 p.m.

Dear God,

Bless me, bless me indeed God! Enlarge my territory (ministry and car sales)! Keep Your hand with me! Keep evil from me, please.

God, Thank You for Your light. I know it's always within me. Sometimes I just feel the need to ask for it. Thank you for the continued re-assurance that it is there.

God, will you please bless me with the sale of the 2003 SL500 that is on our floor. I have two prospects extremely interested. Please bless me with their business. Thank you God. With this sale I look forward to a tithe larger than before 15% instead of 10%. I promise.

Thank you for the confidence to know I deserve this. Thank You for Your blessings, thank You for this day and for Your true love.

❧ You must truly believe that Christ is within you, (after your confession to God of your sins). God is not into bargaining with us as I did above. He wants to bless us daily, as we walk the walk, not just talk the talk. We make promises and break them; God does not.

March 28, 2002   Thursday   9:15 a.m.

Good morning God,

Thank You for waking me this morning! Thank You for giving me the opportunity to share Your Word with my dear friend of many years, Latasha who lives in Los Angeles. Bless her. I know last night's conversation was her plea for You. She struggles with being a man pleaser yet coming further from you God. You used me to comfort her and speak of Your goodness so that she would not feel alone. She can relate to me because I am being delivered from the same bondage at this moment through my gaining of knowledge. Spiritual knowledge. Please use me again and again, I invite You to! Show her Your light daily like I'm seeing it.

But when they deliver you up, do not be anxious about how or what you are to speak; for what you are to say will be given you in that very hour and moment, For it is not you who are speaking, but the Spirit of your Father speaking through you.

Matthew 10:19-20 AMP

When we minister to others, we are more than likely ministering to ourselves. Remember it is our teacher the Holy Ghost speaking, not you.

March 30, 2002   Saturday   8:25 a.m.

Dear God,

Thank You for this morning, thank You for waking me up.

I was met with a challenge this morning; the rental car I have been using while my car is in the shop for maintenance was towed just before my 8:30 a.m. Saturday meeting at work. I parked in back of my apartment and forgot to put my temporary pass in the back window. I even heard You tell me to "go get the pass and bring it back out" when I got home. I learned, of course, what to do next time considering the consequences I'm now facing.

I will not let this incident mold my day. I look forward to all my blessings today, as a righteous child of God (a child in right standing with God, with a repented heart actively seeking Him). I deserve all! I want all! I will stay centered in Christ and listen for guidance all day. Thank You for the words and love You had me send out to my girlfriends and my brother. Please continue to use me.

Now let's go sell some cars today!!!

🌿 The Holy Spirit is our help, even when you forget something. He will remind you if it's for your good.

March 31, 2002   Sunday   6:20 a.m.

"Happy Resurrection Day"

The day Jesus Christ rose from the grave making the Holy Spirit available to us by breaking the curses of sin. Repent for your sins and God will forgive you. The key is you must believe that He forgives you. Work on getting to know the spirit within you, the Holy Spirit.

Dear God,

I ask for Your assistance in my walk with You. I received a call from KG last night. Sometimes we both think and feel that we are going to marry one another, but first we have to be on the same walk; Your walk. I know I've begun my steps, and he is coming closer day by day. He listens and welcomes Your advice and reads Your Word.

This summer he's coming home during his off-season from basketball and expects to date and be with me. Dating him finally involves sincere love (I think). He's tired of the world's disappointments, and is looking forward to things bringing us closer to You God; but if I'm with him, we will fornicate. This is something that KG cannot seem to understand.

Please shine Your light on this challenge God. Make him aware of the things that are right, good, uplifting, peaceful and prosperous in your eyes. Help him choose You over worldly desires.

I appreciate his friendship and feel that he is a friend for a lifetime. Please take this evilness from our friendship. Bring us together the right way – just friends, true friends for the moment. Fornication, please; oh please, remove fornication until marriage, if this is Your will for us. Thank You, God.

Thank You for Your Son, Jesus!

I was asking God to change the thoughts my friend was having, but the bottom line is, I was the one in need of strength to walk with Jesus even while being around a long time companion. I needed prayer and help to flee from sexual sin. I just needed to be honest with myself. I thought I was doing well because I ended sex with him, but I still fell in journal entries to come. To truly walk God's path you must know yourself. You cannot make excuses for the thoughts or actions you have. Rather accept them and seek guidance from the Lord. Be honest with yourself, then God can truly provide.

April 1, 2002　　　　　Monday　　　　　7:25 a.m.

Good Morning God,

Once again I want to thank you for yesterday's importance, the meaning of "the resurrection" of

Jesus. Thank you for the opportunity to be "Born Again," the chance to have the Holy Spirit working in and through me to make all things possible!

I went to visit my brother today in prison and my how he has changed! He has such great wisdom and knowledge of You God. I must say, You sat him down and took him from the evil this world has to offer and filled him with Your light. Thank You for a blessed brother and thank You for a blessed mother. During our visit, we had the best spiritually uplifting conversation ever. We were all aware and on the same page. Keep blessing my family God please!!

Thank You for this day filled with blessings I can't see yet, but I know they are on the way! I love You in the Name of Jesus!!! Amen

Are you ignorant of the fact that all of us who have been baptized into Christ Jesus were baptized into His death ? We are buried therefore with Him by the baptism into death, so that just as Christ was raised from the dead by the glorious (power) of the Father, so we too might (habitually) live and behave in newness of life.

Romans 6:3,4 AMP

🍂 So that our hearts are quickened to desire to live right in God's eyes I will repeat the following: Jesus died and was resurrected (born again) not only to set us free from our past sins, but also to set an example that shows us what we must also do to be in God's presence. (By repeating this message, repetition brings remembrance.) We must be "Born Again." We must die to live.

April 2, 2002   Tuesday   7:40 a.m.

Good Morning God,

I came to this realization several times and now it's dawned on me again; "Is the true reason for journaling a way to capture Your truth and testimonies happening today for a new Bible in a new city to come? The Bible I read today has words and journaling from prophets back in those times, B.C. and after. All of their work composed the Bible. Will You, at the coming of the Lord create another lifetime and use chosen ones' journals for a new Bible to capture the times we are now in, like then?"

God, thank You for sending people who seek comfort. Because I am walking with You, living right, people call me that I haven't heard from in a long time for comfort and for a good Word; they call to receive ministering. Some say they don't even know why they called; they just called. I know its You, Lord sending those that have an ear my way.

Yesterday Mike an old friend, called to tell me about the loss of his mother and how hurt he is. It's been a long time since we last spoke. Thank You for sending him God, I will minister to him today over lunch, uplifting him by sharing Your good news and the Gospel of Jesus.

❧ Just the mention of the name 'Jesus' can bring hope when there seems to be none.

April 3, 2002   Wednesday   1:40 p.m.

Thank You for this day God! Please God, oh please God, bless me with clients without credit problems! Lately, I have been receiving a lot of clients who have challenging credit scores, resulting in loan denials. I know the enemy has stolen from me.

Restore what the enemy has taken.

Please God. Thank you.

And I will restore or replace for you the years that the locust has eaten—the hopping locust, the stripping locust, and the crawling locust, My great army which I sent among you.

Joel 2:25 AMP

For He will give His angels (especial) charge over you to accompany and defend and preserve you in all your ways (of obedience and service).

Psalms 91:11 AMP

❧ Satan will try to steal your joy daily. Just know that as quick as he steals, it is being restored just as speedily as you keep your eyes on Jesus without complaints.

April 8, 2002   Monday   5:20 a.m.

Good morning God, and thank You for providing me with the gift of this morning. Thank You for the Holy Spirit within me made possible by Your Son, Jesus Christ. Thank You.

I want to take this morning to pray for others: my mom; my best friend, Sharon; my brother, Terroll; my friend, Latasha; my friend, Mike; my client, Greg; my grandma, Dorothy Moss; my friend, Tracee; my friend, Natasha; my friend, KG; my friend's daughter, Geneane; my photographer/friend, Ronnie; my client, Evette; my coworker, Joe; my friend, Tony and my manager, Jeff.

Please God in Your Son's name put these people daily in Your light. May they become even more aware of You today, than ever! Use me so that Your will be done!

Knowing that for whatever good anyone does, he will receive his reward from the Lord, whether he is slave or free (believer or non-believer).

Ephesians 6:8 AMP

❦ Prayer for others is our primary assignment as children being taught by God. What we make happen for others God will make happen for us.

<u>April 10, 2002</u>   <u>Wednesday</u>   <u>9:58 p.m.</u>

Good evening God,

I know I have not written in my journal for a couple of days, but I sure have communicated daily through prayer and meditation.

I continue to say, "Thank You for awareness!!" You are truly blessing me daily. I realize if I just continue to obey and remain obedient to Your Words in the Bible I will continue to recognize my blessings.

I have prayed for the last time on my financial state. I do believe and have faith (the two most important words/emotions necessary to acknowledge and receive Your blessings) that You will not only take care of my needs, but You will provide my wants. To receive my wants, I know I must be willing to give something in return. I will list all that I will give in return for Your continued flow of blessings to those around me and myself:

± I gave up my will for Yours God.
± I tithe 10% of my finances to my church whenever You bless me financially (I will do more as You

increase my finances).

± I will continue to go out of my way to be an ear for anyone You send my way.

± I continue to invite You to use me daily to minister Your Words to those who have an ear to hear.

± I will continue to uplift and be a "right" example to those around me, especially my mom.

± I will give the best customer service ever to my Mercedes-Benz clients.

± I will give more to those who send or refer business to me with monetary compensation.

± I will invest to earn interest on my blessings.

± I will consult with you God before all decisions ... how can I go wrong!

🌿 All we must do to continue receiving blessings abundantly is to love God, worship, submit and surrender all to Him. All else will come. We don't have to list what we will do for Him. For it is not by our works that we have been saved, and it surely will not be of our works that will keep us saved. It is the grace of the Almighty God! Manipulation may work in the world, but God is not impressed with it.

I just have to say that the devil is a liar! He tries his best to make us think we are not capable of completing tasks. He also tries to make us think that we are not good enough for riches and wealth because of our past and present sins. All that is negative is of the enemy! I'm here to say I have conquered the enemy through Christ Jesus; no longer can I be persuaded to miss "being" in my anointing and receiving my inheritance from God! I will live right! I will plant only good thoughts in my subconscious mind. For I now know that I, with the strength of the Holy Spirit of Jesus Christ within me, can do all I put my mind to.

First there must be a thought (good for good to manifest); envision it, see it, believe it and then I will put it to action by letting the Holy Spirit guide me. I will force nothing. Things will just happen the way I think they should. It starts with a thought. If I follow these principles, through this flow I will receive all I desire. I must not waver (say one thing and do something else). I must be dedicated in all that I do.

Do not be conformed to this world (this age), (fashioned after and adapted to its external, superficial customs), but be transformed (changed) by the (entire) renewal of your mind (by its new ideals and its new attitude), so that you may prove (for yourselves) what is the good and acceptable and perfect (in His sight for you).

Romans 12:2 AMP

April 12, 2002   Friday   7 p.m.

Dear Father God,

First off, I wanted to thank You for my blessing on Tuesday. On my day off Tony, my brother in Christ and coworker completed a sale for me, and we both prospered $2,000! We both know it was all You!! Thank You.

It seems lately, since my true, right walk with You, I have been journaling a lot about blessings You are sending my way daily. I love this new life that has always been there for the asking. I asked for Your will and not mine, and boy Your will is filled with love, peace, prosperity, continued knowledge, confidence, and true integrity. Thank You for Your way God!

I'd like to take this time to thank You for Tony. Please continue blessing him, his wife, Kim and their children. From day one at my new job, Tony has been a true blessing. I felt he was and still is a guardian angel, a prophet. Today was his last day, *he's moving on to his next assignment, but before he left (oh dear God) he gave me a folder filled with orders he had taken for new car purchases! This folder was filled with great client information necessary to complete his deals. God, through Tony, You have passed onto me a substantial amount of revenue. His clients are now my clients. Thank You God.*

Please bless me daily with Your hand to be of the utmost service to these long time customers of Tony. I appreciate this blessing from You God. Use me! I love You, God.

For by one man's disobedience many were made sinners, so by the obedience of one shall many be made righteous.

Romans 5:19

✤ The choice to walk right in God eyes will be rewarding. As you see in scripture above Adam's wrong choice led to disobedience and consequences that affected the entire world; but on the other hand (God had a second plan) Jesus' right choice to be obedient led to the salvation of all who believe. His choice aligned with the character of God. Obedience is not only the ten-commandments it is also coming in agreement with the Word of God in your everyday living. The Word of God is His character defined and you are the great image of Him. You must desire to walk like, and talk like our great example Jesus for the blessings of God to overflow in your soul. Obedience is the death of your old nature and the life of your new nature in Christ.

April 15, 2002   Monday   9 a.m.

Good Morning Father God,

Thank You for using me in bringing my mother to church service yesterday. She was "Born Again", water baptized and filled with the gift of the Holy Ghost! Hallelujah! I continue to pray for my family's salvation, and as my mother says, "God is using me to get us all there." Thank You. I look forward to what's in store for us. I'm excited with Your grace. My mom is now on her next level, and I believe she's ready with the help of Jesus!

I got a flat tire right after church on the highway, but the enemy could not take my joy away! You are so good to me and sometimes when I tell my friends, I feel like they don't want to hear it. As the Bible says, "Blessed means fortunate, happy, and to be envied." I can't expect those who are not on the same page to want to share in my joy. Please bless me to share with those on the same page and at the right time.

Please bless my friends so can they find salvation in You! Thank You for this day, I look forward to the Holy Spirit guiding me. I love You!

And walk in love, (esteeming and delighting in one another) as Christ loved us and gave Himself up for us, a slain offering and sacrifice to God (for you, so that it became) a sweet fragrance.

Ephesians 5:1-2 AMP

❧ Just being a great example of the Christ that is within can bring souls to the Lord. We must continue to walk the walk, and not just talk the talk. Don't be just a "church-goer" displaying no good fruit of the Lord. Therefore be imitators of God (copy Him and follow His example, Jesus), as well-beloved children (imitate their father).

April 17, 2002   Wednesday   10:20 p.m.

Dear God,

Please give me the scriptures for my mother on sex, for she too struggles with this iniquity. Please God, before satan convinces her that this is not a sin. Thank You.

171

Also, please give me strength to handle all the blessings You are sending me. Thank You. The more I ask for Your blessings the more You send them. You are so awesome!

Tonight Sharon and Tasha, two of my dearest friends, and myself started praying together via phone before going to bed. Please bless this effort to praise You, Father God, nightly. I love You!

Are you so foolish so senseless and so silly? Having begun (your new life spiritually) with the (Holy) Spirit, are you now reaching perfection (by dependence) on the flesh?

Galatians 3:2-3 AMP

Actually, once again 'I' needed these scriptures on sex. I thought at this point I was free from sexual bondage, but I didn't believe it. I still needed to believe that I was truly redeemed from sex (from sin period) because Jesus Christ has already set me free from myself, and its fleshly desires.

❧ Let me ask you this one question: Did you receive the (Holy) Spirit as the result of obeying the Low and doing its works, or was it by hearing (the message of the Gospel) and believing (it)? (Was it from observing a law of rituals or from a message of faith?)

<u>April 22, 2002</u>   <u>Monday</u>   <u>Evening</u>

I always wanted to be different, so I tried different jobs, clothing, hairstyles, men, etc. But this year I truly realized how to be unique and different from the world ... stop sinning like everyone else and live sin free! Now I am different!

Truly I say to you, whoever does not accept and receive and welcome the kingdom of God like a little child (does) shall not in any way enter it (at all).

Luke 18:17 AMP

❧ God has us defined in His Word. His Word is the missing void in our hearts. His Word reveals who we are and who we are meant to be. Don't try to fit into the world's standards being defined by darkness, deceit, and lies. God has made us unique and divinely different. No one of us is the same therefore we need to stop trying to be so. Identical twins may share the same DNA, but have a unique difference; their fingerprints and that's it! Become a child again and let the Holy Spirit teach you about who you really are. A child of the Living God!

April 23, 2002 Tuesday 8:10 a.m.

Good Morning God,

Thank You for this day. Thank You for the strength to get up and workout daily in Your Word and in the gym.

She girds herself with strength (spiritual, mental, and physical fitness for her God-given task) and makes her arms strong and firm.

Proverbs 31:17

Dear Father God thank You for using me these past two Sundays to bring souls to You. Last Sunday my mom joined me at church, and she was filled with the gift of the Holy Ghost, born-again and baptized in the name of Jesus. This Sunday I picked her up and she asked if a couple of other ladies could join us. Of course I said yes. During this service one of the young ladies, Jennifer, was filled with the Holy Ghost, born-again and baptized in the Name of Jesus. Thank You for using my mom and myself. Keep on! I welcome You.

Thank You Father God for the people you have blessed me with to sell cars to this month. I prayed to You to pay off some debts I owed from my past, and You have blessed me with buying clients. Thank You Jesus. Thank You God. I know I deserve all Your blessings because I am Your righteous child.

Thank You Father God for the words to tell KG that our relationship could never be what it used to be: sex, dishonesty, and nothing that was right. He was anxious to start a relationship that had trust, honesty, and integrity, but not without sex. So ... Oh well, we will be friends and build on that. He understood as I stated, "I choose God and living right over him (this world) any day!" He is not worth me sinning and missing some of my blessings. No way!

God, please continue to bless our friendship, use me to open KG's eyes to the many blessings of being obedient. May we grow together or grow apart. May Your will God be done.

Thank You God for Your anointing on my life. I will not let the evil one take my crown!

Therefore if any person is (ingrafted) in Christ (the Messiah) he is a new creation (a new creature altogether); the old (previous moral and spiritual condition) has passed away. Behold the fresh and new has come!

2 Corinthians 5:17 AMP

❧ As we recognize the newness of life, and who we really are in Christ Jesus, we are eager to renounce the past and look forward.

April 26, 2002   Friday   7:03 a.m.

Good Morning Father God!

Thank You for answered prayer! Thank You for a praying mother. Thank You for a blessed month at work. I prayed for $8,000 to settle debts and You blessed me with $10,000 so far from my car sales. Hallelujah! Now that I am more responsible with my money, I know that I must tithe first. Then I must pay my debts (if any), save or invest some, and give wherever You lead me. At this point you will continue to bless me financially. Thank You for lessons learned.

Father God, bless my best friend Sharon and whatever challenges she may be facing. Sometimes I feel like she is not as happy for me with my spiritual growth as she shows. She was a true stepping stone for my awareness, and I continuously thank her. I thank You, God. We can both continue to learn from one another. When I talk of the gift of the Holy Ghost with the evidence of speaking in tongues, she doesn't seem too happy for my new awareness. It seems like she was more pleased when I needed her to share Your Word to me, as I seeked Your guidance. Please God bless our friendship and give me the right words at the right time. I do love her and appreciate her and all that she has done with Your guidance.

I realize it's hard for those that have helped you to become more aware of God to let go, and know, now, that You have taken over from that point. There are some things that I have experienced quickly that my spiritual friends have not. Please allow them to be happy for me and not envious. Just because you have been in the church longer or in the Word longer, doesn't mean a new "born again" Christian can't experience wonderful things more swiftly than other "church-going" Christians. I want all Your gift's God!

But the manifestation of the Spirit is given to every man to profit withal. — For to one is given by the Spirit the word of wisdom; to another the word of knowledge by the same Spirit; — To another faith by the same Spirit; to another the gifts of healing by the same Spirit; — To another the working of miracles; to another discerning of spirits; to another divers kinds of tongues; to another the interpretation of tongues: — But all these worketh that one and the self-same Spirit, dividing to every man severally as he will (AS HE CHOOSES).

1 Corinthians 12:7-11

❧ God is more than able to quicken our growth in Him therefore bringing us into the fullness of the spiritual gifts that He so freely has for those who "choose" to believe.

April 29, 2002   Monday   9:01 a.m.

Dear Father God,

Thank You for this day! Thank You for life! You said in Isaiah 54:17, "No weapon formed against thee shall prosper ..." Bless all those that come across my path even if they do not have good intentions for me. Bless my general manager, fill his spirit with good,

for he is ignorant at this moment, bless him.
My Sundays are filled with studying Your Word, so by Monday the enemies attempt to steal my focus is on! Please guide me through this day with no pressure, just grace. Please God, bless Eddie with the strength and energy to get his purchase paperwork back to me before "end-of-month," so his sale will count for this month. Do this for me God. Thank You. Bless my mom with the new job she claimed today! Thank You. Let us overcome any test we may be faced with today. For the evil one is not happy that yesterday he received no attention. He will not receive it today! I love You, Father God!!!

Father, I realize that I have to let go of things that have consumed my past, and patiently wait for what you have for the present. Half of what I had in the past, before being saved, was given to me by the enemy; so I must let it go, and You will show me what You have for me. I must step out on faith!!!!!!

God, I pray for an aggressive spirit at my job. The more sales I make, the more I can tithe, give, and help the way You want me to. In Jesus' Name bless me; oh bless me indeed, with this aggressive spirit to maximize the opportunities You have blessed me with.

I ask that we (You and I) sell 15 cars a month for the remainder of the year. In Jesus' name, Amen.

While anyone is hearing the Word of the kingdom and does not grasp and comprehend it, the evil one comes and snatches away what was sown in his heart. This is what was sown along the roadside.

Matthew 13:19

Study to show thyself approved unto God, a workman that needeth not to be ashamed, rightly dividing the word of truth.

2 Timothy 2:15

🌿 Once the teaching is received on Sundays the enemy comes to steal the Word from us immediately. We must stay in the Word, study the Word, meditate on the Word, and receive revelation on the Word to keep it. This is where our true 'knowing' of our freedom comes.

May 7, 2002   Tuesday   10:15 a.m.

Dear Father God,

I bless You and praise You, bless and praise Jesus; thank You for life!

I have realized, thanks to You God, that it is a challenge to try to get my old relationships to accept the new me. It can slow down my awareness growth because I'm trying so hard to get others to know the new, righteous me. Stop!! I will from this day forward, invite new relationships into my life to continue my spiritual awareness without any difficulties. These new friends could possibly be God-sent to help keep me where I am and help me to my next spiritual level.

Thank You for my past God, but hallelujah to my present and future. I must look ahead.

Let your light so shine before men that they may see your moral excellence and your praiseworthy, noble, and good deeds and recognize and honor and praise and glorify your Father Who is in heaven.

Matthew 5:16

❧ Once a Christian, we should not try to convince others of our walk. We will glow without shining the searchlight on those who do not yet believe.

May 9, 2002   Thursday   10:06 p.m.

Dear Father God,

I praise, magnify and glorify Your name. Thank You God for Your Son, Jesus Christ. Thank You for making it possible for me through the Holy Spirit to be all that Jesus is! A great expression of You! Thank You, God for answered prayer. I pray daily for You to send someone to me who is seeking ministry of Your Word. Today You sent Veronica. She said that she just felt the desire in her heart to call me because things are not right in her life. She needed someone to talk to, someone positive. Thank You God for using me; please continue to use me in guiding her to You.

Also, Father God, thank You for Antonio (a friend from church). I finally think you are part/all of the reason he has made himself known. He knows and loves You. Is he the one You sent for me? Bless us.

But seek (aim at and strive after) first of all His kingdom and His righteousness (His way of doing and being right), and then all these things taken together will be given you besides.

Matthew 6:33 AMP

❧ We're always wondering if someone is "the one," and not completely seeking the Lord first and only. For we must know that the Lord is preparing us for whom He will have find us. We must fall deeply in Love with Him first, before we can "sincerely" fall deeply in Love with a human companion and be true. Jesus is our first mate.

May 16, 2002   Thursday   Noon

Dear Father God,

Thank You for this day. Thank You for answered prayers.

My mother's back living with me due to the negative influences around her, and through faith in You God, I know there is good in this situation. She has to stay focused on you Lord with no distractions. I will continue to be a great example for her through Your grace. She is a new child growing in You, with no limitations just as I am. Please bless her with her own apartment/home and her own car. Use me to make this happen. Thank You God, in Jesus' Name. Amen.

Also, thank You, Father God for a man of you, Antonio. I do not know if he is in my life for a reason, season or a lifetime. We pray together, love and glorify Your name together, respect each other, listen to each other, laugh all the time, and are both morning persons. You said in Your Word a man findeth a good woman. (A good thing.) Bless and anoint our union. May I receive all the blessings and awareness you have for me in this friendship. Please allow Antonio to receive the same blessings. Please continue to shape and mold us to be all we can be with Your love, in Jesus' name. Amen.

He Who descended is the (very) same as He Who also has ascended high above all the heavens, that He (His presence) might fill all things (the whole universe, from the lowest to the highest).

Ephesians 4:10

⚜ We continue to seek to fill a void in our lives when the real void is within. The complete fulfillment is made aware once Christ is within. All voids are filled when we are filled with the Spirit of Love, God.

May 24, 2002   Friday   8:30 p.m.

Dear Father God,

Thank You for Your goodness, Your greatness, Your blessings, and Your love!!

Your love is so kind. I'm crying at this very moment because You are so good to me. I have seen my finances grow, my friendships build, and my family grow in spiritual awareness.

God, You are so big in my life! There is nothing bigger than You!

My life is the best it has ever been. Thank You, God. I know there is more to come.

Thank You God also for the Trinity Broadcast Network (TBN)! Please keep this Christian television network going.

Thank You for being the best friend I always had, but didn't know it.

Thank you, God for the strength of Your son Jesus

Christ in me. You blessed me with a second month earnings of $15,000!! Thank You for making a young lady (me) that is new to the business prosper so quickly. I know it's all You. I look forward to more. Tithing first of course!!!

Please use me to spread Your good news. Please continue to bless my memory on good things. I can sing for You, minister for You, dance for You. How do You want me to do it?

Thank (God) in everything (no matter what the circumstances my be, be thankful and give thanks), for this is the will of God for you (who are) in Christ Jesus (the Revealer and Mediator of that will).

1 Thessalonians 5:18 AMP

❧ We should thank the Lord always for how he blesses us and has met our needs. But, more importantly we should thank Jesus for freeing us from our sins, making the Holy Spirit available to us, not only through his death on the cross but his resurrection (his example of the importance of being born again) has brought us into relationship with the Kingdom of God.

Tracy L. Moss

<u>May 26, 2002</u>   Sunday   <u>7:18 a.m.</u>

Good morning Father God!!

You are my Father, my Husband, my Friend, my Love and my Life. Thank You for our relationship.

Dear precious Father put the man in my life that You know will take care of me the way You do. There are several men trying to be in my life, all with wonderful words, financial security, looks, and kindness. Guide me God. You are in control of my life. Please help me to cause no pain. Thank You in Jesus' name for answered prayer. Amen.

Bless all my family, friends, and enemies on this day. May I receive all the blessings You have for me. It's Your promise, as I obey Your Word. Love, Tracy

❧ I'm lovin' on the Lord more and more daily as I study and read His Word. But, I still have not reached the place of being whole and complete in Him. I have never been single, never without a boyfriend. The Lord really desires for me to concentrate on Him and Him only, and not "Now that I'm walking with you Oh, Lord when will my companion that you have chosen find me?"

For your Maker is your Husband—the Lord of hosts is His name…and the Holy One of Israel is your Redeemer; the God of the whole earth He is called.

Isaiah 54:5

🌿 We must accept the truth that God has our perfect mate ready to present to us in His time. Until then Jesus is our spiritual husband. Jesus will take us with all our "old baggage" with no complaints, only Love.

June 4, 2002   Tuesday   7:30 p.m.

Dear Father God, I love You, and I magnify Your name! You are so powerful and of great influence. I adore You.

It has been put on my heart to journal about a challenge I'm experiencing. I do know I'll continue to have challenges in this new walk because until You come for me, I will always need You. I can do nothing without You. My challenge is men. I am no longer intimate (sex), but I continue to meet men and like them. They are aware of You, but I always find something wrong with them and move on to the next. It's not good, because they usually care for me more than I care for them. Being blessed with beauty, inside and out, attracts great guys, but why can't I attract one that I'm completely satisfied with?

I know why (revelation while writing) ...

You are not done with me, and my attention should be on You and doing my best to get to know You, God. I know You will bless me with the man You want in my life. Please continue to guide me with friends (just friends) so I may not cause pain or feel pain. You are my number one priority and all else will fall into place when the time is right, per Your will. Thank You Father!

But when the complete and perfect (total) comes, the incomplete and imperfect will vanish away (become antiquated, void, and superseded).

1 Corinthians 13:10 AMP

He has made everything beautiful in its time. He also has planted eternity in men's hearts and minds (a Divinely implanted sense of a purpose working through the ages which nothing under the sun but God alone can satisfy), yet so that men cannot find out what God has done from the beginning to the end.

Ecclesiastes 3:11 AMP

🌿 The peace of God transcends all understanding once we become aware of the deepest need in us. Christ is the presence of God in us, the only presence that will bring complete satisfaction.

Blessing

I asked and prayed that my general manager be disciplined for always giving me a hard time. His spirit is not of You, God, and we were experiencing strife because my spirit is of You. I prayed for assistance and let go instead of letting the same spirit that was controlling him control my actions and reactions. I showed him love, the exact opposite of what he expected. I obeyed Your Word Father, "Love your enemies."

Within a few days of doing it Your way God, I came in one morning to find the general manager in my office having my name monogrammed on the front glass. He smiled and politely said, "This is how you want your named spelled, right?" This let me know he was officially welcoming me to his team. God is good!! "My enemies will be under my feet, I already have victory over all obstacles! Obey My Words and Your enemies will become your footstools."

Now, I get nothing but smiles, and respect from my general manager because I showed integrity, respect and discipline. Mostly I showed him "Love."

But the fruit of the (Holy) Spirit (the work which His presence within accomplishes) is love, joy (gladness), peace, patience (an even temper, forbearance), kindness, goodness (benevolence), faithfulness, gentleness (meekness, humility), self-control (self-restraint, continence). Against such there is no law (that can bring charge). And those who belong to Christ Jesus (the Messiah) have crucified the flesh (the godless human nature) with its passions and appetites and desires. If we live by the (Holy) Spirit, let us also walk by the Spirit. (If by the Holy Spirit we have our life in God, let us go forward walking in line, our conduct controlled by the Spirit.)

Galatians 5:22-25 AMP

God's nature is not one of strife. The minute you decide to step out of the comfort of the fruits of the Holy Spirit you will lose the anointing of God (His presence). No misunderstanding is worth it! Don't let your flesh take control with evidence of your old nature (old self and it's world defined ways that have kept you in bondage). Stay in the Spirit and God will be in control. The battle does not have to be yours if you call on the Lord!

June 8, 2002   Sunday   8 p.m.

Dear Father God,

Thank You for this Sunday! Thank You for Your blessing of Love! Thank You for loving me with all my
iniquities (my sins). For I know I'm not strong
enough by myself to resist temptation, but I know as
I grow in Your Word I can with Jesus' help, by my
Holy Spirit.

God bless KG he needs you, so do I! Bless our friendship to grow however You want it to. My life is in
Your hands.

Here are my visions:
± To receive love as I give love.
± To receive truth, honesty, and integrity as I give
and display it.
± To be a great example through Your Word.
± To minister/evangelize to those suffering from this
world, including myself.

And the Lord answered me and said, 'Write the vision and
engrave it so plainly upon tablets ... For the vision is yet for
an appointed time and it hastens to the end (fulfillment); it
will not deceive or disappoint.'

Habakkuk 2:2-3a AMP

🌿 As we believe in the unseen it is important to write down our visions and watch them come into manifestation. In God's time not ours.

June 11, 2002   Tuesday   10 p.m.

Blessing

Dear Father God,

Thank You for using me to direct souls closer to You so they may receive the gift of the Holy Spirit through Christ Jesus!

My mom called me today from work to just thank me for her change. Of course she recognizes that it's not of me that good works were done, but of the Father using me to get to her. Thank You God. Please keep using me!

Also, I received a call from KG thanking me for his birthday present, a tape series by Joyce Meyers. The Holy Spirit led me to order these tapes for him to *help with his inability to forgive. I also prayed that he would receive them with an open ear and heart. He said that it was the best present ever! He's coming God! Use me more to bring him to You. I love You God.*

But when they deliver you up, do not be anxious about how or what you are to speak; for what you are to say will be given you in that very hour and moment, For it is not you who are speaking, but the Spirit of your Father speaking through you.

Matthew 10:19-20 AMP

❧ The Holy Spirit wants to use us, that our Father in Heaven may get all the glory. Do not fret when this moment comes, the Holy Spirit will give you what to say.

June 18, 2002   Tuesday   6:15 a.m.

Dear Father God,

Thank You for forgiveness, truth, awareness, and Your inheritance for me! Thank You for my mother! Thank You for my friends! Thank You for my feet, hands, body, eyes, lips, hair and teeth! Thank You for Love!!

God please continue to give me strength at my job. I realize I need more product knowledge; I haven't received any more "new sales" training since I've been here (at least no formal training). I know with and through Christ Jesus I will be guided to the studies I need and with experiences to learn from. Please God help me to finish up this month's goals set before me. (No goal was given to me from management this month, but I know it is 10 cars) Although, I've only been here for four months I know I have a goal consistent with someone who's been selling for a year, but I can do it with Christ who strengthens me of course.

Thank You, Father God for using me to help get KG closer to You through Your positive Word (scriptures) and tapes. As he moves onto the next level of getting to know You, I realize Your work through me is done, for now. Bless him in his journey with lessons to be learned; also may he love with all his heart.

It is time for my personal life to take on new rela-

tionships. I see how You are ending the old, and making way for new experiences. I am a better person today than yesterday as I continue to grow in Your Word and I thank You. I love myself; therefore I can truly love others, respect others, be true to others and just be myself. I realize when You have the Holy Spirit within You, when You believe, people are attracted to your inner more instantly than your outer. Praise God!!!

I do not consider, brethren, that I have captured and made it my own (yet); but one thing I do (it is my one aspiration); forgetting what lies behind and straining forward to what lies ahead.

Philippians 3:13 AMP

🌿 Press forward, leave the past behind keeping your mind on Christ Jesus for renewal. Meditate on His Word. If the past is calling you on the phone right now and is not speaking the wisdom of God—hang up! The newness and hope of life is the focus! Keep your eyes on Jesus!

June 20, 2002   Thursday   9:45 p.m.

Dear God, first, thank You for the blessings today, thank You!!

Father God, my heart is heavy ... The more and more I think my friendship with KG has finally come to an end, the more I feel You are not done using me to bring him closer to you. Yes, I do love him and truly desire for him to be saved, but it doesn't seem possible for us to just "be friends" and walk a spiritual walk together. Every time we are around one another, I love him more and just want to be someone he can count on and trust. But lustful desires lead us to become intimate with one another, and this is what makes having a "friendship" harder. I think it's a challenge because we dated for almost five years.

So many times, KG has called me with his last name attached to mine, and I don't know if you want me to hang in there and be the great example he needs. He wants me to just wait for him and witness his change, but there's no commitment to each other, and we both still have other friends. It doesn't seem like he can accept the fact that he is not the only one I'm seeing even though I accept it with him.

God, are you done using me for KG? Have I not tried hard enough to hang in there no matter what and let you continue to use me? Is this my future *[mate]? Will I have a future testimony of the challenges experienced in our relationship?*

I don't know why my heart is heavy. I just feel like You still need me for his spiritual growth, I can live with not being future companions if this is Your will. But, I would love to help bring a soul to You. Use me and guide me. Let KG feel and know that I am here for him. Guide him to church with me or just to church. Thank You.

Bring him back if it is Your will as we depart from one another, due to the fact it's too difficult to be near each another without sin interrupting. Remove sin from us, in Jesus' name. Amen.

What harmony can there be between Christ and Belial (the devil)? Or what has a believer in common with an unbeliever?
2 Corinthians 6:14-15 AMP

My people are destroyed for lack of knowledge: because thou hast rejected knowledge...
Hosea 4:6a

❧ Being unequally yoked is not just for married couples, but also those in relationships. The believer and non-believer have nothing in common. When dating a man or woman that is not walking with Christ in them, that individual is still seeking satisfaction in a world that is not meant to satisfy. This individual can never be completely satisfied. He too must fill his inner void as a believer has, to be filled with true love to love another sincerely. Only hurt, and confusion will result in this type of relationship. Do not be unequally yoked with unbelievers (do not make mismated alliances with them or come under a different yoke with them, inconsistent with your faith). For what partnership have right living and right standing with God with iniquity and lawlessness? Or how can light fellowship with darkness?

June 24, 2002   Monday   12:10 a.m.

Dear Father God, my Best Friend, my True Love, my Everything, my All, my Provider, my Strength, my Source, my All, my Lover, my Protector, my All, I love You, praise You, and magnify Your name. Thank You for being!!

Blessing

Thank You God for fulfilling the goals I have made for myself at Mercedes. You have blessed me and enabled me to be named "top salesperson" this past Saturday when I sold three cars in one day, earning me an extra bonus of $500! I know it was all You, show-

ing me that if I believe I can do all things through You, because I am the great expression of You. What a wonderful gift You have graced me with through Your Son, Jesus Christ. Thank You once again!

Father God You are so true to Your Word found in the Bible. Each day I see the truth unfolding with the help of the Holy Spirit within me. As I tithe my first fruits weekly I continue to see prosperity in every way, especially in my finances. Thank You God for guiding me to the right messages from Your disciples (pastors), spiritual tapes, and to the right scriptures in the Bible. For it is truly necessary for my spirit to be nurtured toward peace, good health, prosperity, and most of all love daily!!

Bring all the tithes (the whole tenth of your income) into the storehouse, that there may be food in My house, and prove Me now by it, says the Lord of hosts, if I will not open the windows of heaven for you and pour you out a blessing, that there shall not be room enough to receive it.

Malachi 3:10 AMP

❧ Tithing is an act of obedience. God has commandments and statues for our good, not to punish us. Obedience is the key to the prosperity of our souls, then our outer circumstances. Being obedient is following His commandments, His wisdom, His ways. Walk in Godly wisdom, not worldly wisdom.

Dear Father God,

Thank You for this day, thank You for any challenges this day may bring, thank You for the Holy Spirit to handle and overcome anything! The devil is a liar!!! You Lord, Oh God are the truth!!!!!!

May "Your will" continue to be done in the life you have graced and blessed me with. Thank You for favor. In Jesus' Name, Amen!! Amen!!

Consider it wholly joyful, my brethren, whenever you are enveloped in or encounter trials of any sort or fall into various temptations. Be assured and understand that the trial and proving of your faith bring out endurance and steadfastness and patience. But let endurance and steadfastness and patience have full play and do a thorough work, so that you may be (people) perfectly and fully developed (with no defects), lacking in nothing.

James 1:2-4 AMP

❧ Daily confirmations are good; they prepare you for trials. Reading the Word on a daily basis helps to strengthen your awareness and knowledge of the Christ within. Many agree, God's compassion never fails; that He is faithful and His mercy never ceases. It is the testing of your faith that develops perseverance.

July 15, 2002   Monday   6:58 a.m.

Dear Father God,

Thank You, first off, for this day that You have blessed me with! Thank You for continued peace in the midst of storm! God, Your many different messengers continue to pull me towards Romans, Chapter 7; "A Christian struggling." I'd like to share my story with anyone experiencing similar situations in their lives. So they may receive a message from You, but these people have yet to present themselves. So, I must put it in my journal and wait on You to work it out God.

I am a Christian struggling with the sin of sexual lust. I need help, this has been part of my past failures and is now manifesting in my new "Born Again" life. I need it to stop now, God! Deep within my heart I only want to be intimate with my hus-

band, according to Your will. I have always thought that "making love" is part of a relationship, but when that relationship doesn't work out, then I feel I have shared too much of me.

Also, sex has shown me negative consequences. Men are in love with me, but I don't know if it's love or lust. I have two men in my life who talk about marriage, and I do feel that they have love for me, but I think I make it worse when I become intimate. God, I want one mate, one love, one God-sent. Help me to choose what steps to take next:

Focus on my relationship with You and let You guide my steps. Let You, God, bring me strength, and let You, God, change my iniquities through your Holy Spirit.   Yes, Yes, Yes!!

Bless KG, and our longtime relationship. I do love and care for him a lot and would love for him to have a personal relationship with Christ Jesus. With this relationship, he would understand me more and trust me. It's a challenge for him to trust me because of the way I used to be. He hasn't gotten truly acquainted with the new Tracy in Christ Jesus. Is it meant for me to give in or up?

🌿 God has not imparted in believers a spirit to give-up, but a spirit of steadfast endurance to run the Christian race. This gift should not be used to stay in a relationship that is unequally yoked. Giving in would satisfy satan's plan for my life and not God's plan.

Bless Mark, my year-and-a-half relationship. I have deep love for him and need him to be saved from his own self-destruction. He needs to understand he can come to Jesus just the way he is. He has visions of being a man of Truth and his mom even told him, before she passed, he would become a preacher. I know he wants change in his life. Sometime I feel like he, out of all the men I've dated, can most definitely love me with all his heart and not want for anyone else. God, do You have me in his life to bless him with love so that he may do good works for Your glory? If so let me know, please!!!!!

Also, Lord bless my new friend Kenny who knows You, praises You, and respects me. I just have to respect myself. Kenny is a carnal Christian who grew up in a church, but hasn't given his life completely over to the Holy Spirit to guide him. Should I let go of the old Tracy's past relationships, and try this new one?

God I know it is not of You that I am confused so I rebuke it now! I will trust in You, Lord, to continue to take me down a path of righteousness. No questions asked or complaints concerning any outcomes.

God, You are great!! I will wait and listen.

For God is not the author of confusion, but of peace, as in all churches of the saints.

1 Corinthians 14:33

And when the devil had ended every (the complete cycle of) temptation, he temporarily left Him (that is, stood off from him) until another more opportune and favorable time.

Luke 4:13 AMP

❧ Notice the repetition of satan's tactics. He focuses his attacks on our weakest areas (areas that we are in doubt of). Pay attention to your first intuition (God's wisdom); that quiet voice within your heart, the quirky, almost uneasy feeling, in your stomach that things are not right! These are your warnings! Give the Holy Spirit attention! Obey, God!

July 16, 2002   **Tuesday**   **2:30 p.m.**

To anyone who reads this, God is a good God! He is all good!!!!!

O' Taste and see that the Lord is good: blessed is the man that trusts in him.

Psalms 34:8

And they answered, Believe in the Lord Jesus Christ (give yourself up to Him, take yourself out of your own keeping and entrust yourself into His keeping) and you will be saved, (and this applies both to) you and your household as well.

Acts 16:31

❧ Be renewed daily in Spirit, mind, then body with God's wisdom. Read the Word daily, confess the Word, think on things that are good and true in the eyes of God. Praising Him lifts your spirit!

July 19, 2002   **Friday**   **8:15 p.m.**

Dear Heavenly Father God,

I bless, praise, adore, love, and magnify Your name! You are amazing, You are great, You are loving, You are merciful, and I thank You for Your grace.

God, please forgive me of my sins today, and thank You for forgetting them. Thank You.

I do realize that no matter how much You forgive me for my past sins, consequences still follow. Eventually, I will get to a point where I can consciously know what type of consequence will result according to a particular sin, and I will not do it. I'm working on it with the strength of the Holy Spirit within me. Day by day, I realize how much You love me and bless me no matter what. I am growing to love You the same. I am continuing to strive to please You and not this world. For I know when I do this, my entire life will be all peace. No condemnation from sin, all peace. A life focused on saying "no" to the world's temptations will bring me these results:

± Sex with my husband will be peaceful; no "world presented" disappointments we can't work out together, because we will go to our Father, God.
± Honest and true people will continually enter my life.
± Prosperity and growth in my career.

± *Family peace.*

± *The opportunity of a lifetime to be used completely by You as a motivator, an evangelist to all who do not know the Truth, Jesus.*

± *Help to bring souls to You, Father.*

Thank you for choosing me God!!

Now if (all these things are true, then be sure) the LORD knows how to rescue the godly out of temptations and trials, and how to keep the ungodly under chastisement until the day of judgment and doom.

2 Peter 2:9

🌿 Choosing what is not of God will bring on consequences of itself. Living by God's wisdom and obeying them will bring only "good" results. This is why you must know the wisdom of God so that you may align with it for better results to your choices. God's Word says that many are called, but few are chosen. I realized that our Father calls for all, but not all that are called will choose Him. God has no favorites all can experience His true peace. (Matthew 22:14)

July 20, 2002   Saturday   Morning

Dear Father God,

I have asked that You bless my friendship with my
new friend Kenny. I know that You have, but no
matter how much we both know You and magnify Your
name, still lustful thoughts come upon us.
I really believe that he is an awesome person. We
even like watching cartoons together. I love the kid
in him, but I know I can't continue to do the very
things You don't want me to do. Initially when I met
Kenny I said this relationship would be different.
Yes, he was another athlete, but this would be different. I was now a "Born Again" woman of God, and
I would stand my ground regardless of the temptations placed in my path. I told him I was not interested in being intimate, at all.

We spent time together, daily, thus we were becoming more and more attracted to one another. We were
"feeling" each other a lot. It happened. Sex entered
into our friendship and guilt followed. He did not
seem to feel like I did about this sin. The main thing
that touched me was a cross with Jesus on it hang-
ing above his bed. For I knew Jesus was no longer

on that cross, and I knew deep inside I was wrong. I was out of the Will of God. I was having sex, and I was having it under a cross. Please forgive me, Father.

Before this intimacy occurred in the past few weeks, I went into the bathroom and prayed for strength to say no. I asked for the Holy Spirit to come and stop it. But I ended up still giving in. I know it wasn't that this man was so irresistible. It was the cunning attempts of satan and my choosing my worldly desires over God's desires for me.

I finally hit the ultimate conviction. No more sex. No more sex. I must stop. This time I had gone into the bathroom to pray for strength and came out only to cave into my fleshy desires. This time when I looked up at the cross with Jesus on it I felt something. I don't know what it was but when we got out of the bed after satisfying ourselves, it was filled with blood. Not just spots but filled with blood. No, it was not that time of the month for me. (I cry as I continue to write) I knew God was trying to tell me something. He had given me a "sign!" I went home that day and cried out to Jesus to save me from *this!!! End the relationship or make changes, please. Was I being reminded of the blood that Jesus shed to free me from this very sin? From all sin?*

MY LITTLE CHILDREN, I write you these things so that you may not violate God's law and sin. But if anyone should sin we have an Advocate (One Who will intercede for us) with the Father- (it is) Jesus Christ (the all) righteous (upright, just, Who conforms to the Father's will in every purpose, thought, and action). — And He (that same Jesus Himself) is the propitiation (the atoning sacrifice) for our sins, and not for ours alone but also for (the sins of) the whole world.

1 John 2:1-2

Know, recognize, and understand therefore that the Lord your God, He is God, the faithful God, Who keeps covenant and steadfast love and mercy with those who love Him and keep His commandments, to a thousand generations.

Deuteronomy 7:9 AMP

✣ God used this as yet another learning experience, designed to renew "awareness" of disobedience. Conviction by the Holy Spirit brings on change. Conviction is not meant to continue the act of repentance over and over again. But, oh, thank God for His mercy!

<u>July 28, 2002</u>   Sunday   <u>3:45 p.m.</u>

Dear Father God,

I just want to take this precious moment You have blessed me with, to give You thanks. Thank You for my mom, my brother, my great health, my great new friends: Kenny, Tony and his family, Joseph and his family. Thank You for my job, thank You for the challenges on my job and the answered prayers of guidance and the ability to conquer them. Thank You for taking care of my needs and fulfilling some of my wants (if they are Your will), thanks for the Holy Spirit, thank You for the Bible, thank You for a personal relationship with You through Jesus, thank You for protection against the enemy, thank You for the knowing that no weapon formed against me shall prosper. Thank You for showing me true love! Thank You for the realization that without Jesus, Your Son, I can do nothing. Thank You for the favor and grace to be a chosen one, to be made daily into the great expression of You just as Jesus was while living in this world. Thank You God for the Holy Ghost, to act as an intercessor keeping me on track. Thank You for goals that are always reachable through faith. Thank You for the spirit of commitment, the spirit of love, the spirit of truth, the spirit of honesty, the spirit of integrity, the spirit of peace, the spirit of satisfaction, the spirit of forgiveness, the spirit of a cheerful giver, the spirit of discernment, the spirit of love; the spirit of You!!!

Especially thank You for the spirit of patience and steadfast endurance to not give up! I love You God in Jesus' name, Amen!!!!!!

A time will come, however, indeed it is already here, when the true (genuine) worshipers will worship the Father in spirit and in truth (reality); for the Father is seeking just such people as these as His worshipers. — God is a Spirit (a spiritual being) and those who worship Him must worship Him in spirit and truth (reality).

John 4:23-24 AMP

✤ Let God share your joy! Let Him into every area of your life! Keep in touch with Him through praise and worship, thanking Him in all you say and do; giving Him the Glory! Seek Him continuously, in your life; as though He were a "rare" gem! After all, He is!

July 31, 2002   Wednesday   Morning

Dear God,

You are so amazing; how You save us from ourselves when we ask!

My friend Kenny has been traded to a team in another state, a state far from Chicago. I wasn't sad because I know, God, that this is Your will and You are going to do great things for the both of us. Thank You Father for saving me from continued sin, thank You for saving us both. Please bless Kenny with his new team, may he strive to grow stronger in Your Word. I know I surely will. I do not think this is the end of our friendship, but for now it is.

I LOVE the Lord, because He has heard (and now hears) my voice and my supplications. — Because He has inclined His ear to me, therefore will I call upon Him as long as I live.
                                        Psalms 116:1-2 AMP

And my God will liberally supply (fill to the full) your every need according to His riches in glory in Christ Jesus.
                                        Philippians 4:19 AMP

But, on the contrary, as the Scripture says, What eye has not seen and ear has not heard and has not entered into the heart of man, (all that) God has prepared (made and keeps ready) for those who love Him (who hold Him in affectionate reverence, promptly obeying Him and gratefully recognizing the benefits He has bestowed).

1 Corinthians 2:9 AMP

✺ Be careful for what you ask in prayer! Specify to our Father God, your desires; but keep it simple! God already knows your needs, as well as your desires. He hears your cry!

August 1, 2002   Thursday   8:30 p.m.

Thank you God for the Trinity Broadcast Network (TBN) this station has truly helped to take me to another level of spirituality. I watch it daily and my spirit is nurtured and strengthened. Thank you God.

Dear Heavenly Father also thank You for the blessing and desire to pursue golfing. I know with Christ, I can do all things and that is my only hope. After only four lessons my beginning and end stance, amazed my instructor. I look forward to excelling; my new goal is to start competing. Thank You God for a life filled with peace and abundant joy!

Father, thank You for sending customers and managers to me that are Christians. I know You will send both for me to serve, but I feel so at peace and at home when I'm assisting them.

Tuesday, on my day off, I was going golfing but since it was the end of the month I prayed to You to see if I should go in and try to sell car number nine for the month. You (God) guided me to go in to work, I thought I was there merely checking my messages, but while I was checking them my manager walked in and asked me if I wanted to help a customer. Oh Dear God, the customer was a Christian Pastor! She was in the dealership just for service on her 1999 E-Class and as a true blessing (through Your help God) I was able to help her trade in her car for a newer model Mercedes, a 2002 S-Class. She truly felt that You had sent me to serve her on my day off. She had actually been in prayer for a new "upgrade." We thanked You sincerely for our meeting!!!!

Father I have been in prayer about a trip to Jamaica for a friend's wedding. I'd be going with old friends, including my ex-boyfriend, Mark. We'd even discussed this trip previously when we were *together. It seems the way has been made clear for my departure. Goals have been made at work, and I have had no thoughts of struggle concerning taking this trip. It seems so right, and I feel You have something for me to do for You during my trip. Use me, Oh Lord. Let me minister; let me share Your truth while I'm in Jamaica. Thank You Father for the comfort I feel with this decision. Keep me safe from evil so that I may not cause pain or feel pain.*

Blessed (happy, blithesome, joyous, spiritually prosperous — with life-joy and satisfaction in God's favor and salvation, regardless of their outward conditions) are the meek (the mild, patient, long-suffering), for they shall inherit the earth!

Matthew 5:5 AMP

May the God of your hope so fill you with all joy and peace in believing (through the experience of your faith) that by the power of the Holy Spirit you may abound and be overflowing (bubbling over) with hope.

Romans 15:13 AMP

❧ The LORD takes pleasure in His people. He increases their blessings; uplifting and beautifying their lives. He does this by restoring our souls first.

August 9, 2002   Friday   10:30 a.m.

Montego Bay, Jamaica

Dear Heavenly Father,

First thank You for salvation, thank You for saving me form this world I live in. Thank You for Your Son Jesus Christ!

I am here in Jamaica. Already, several temptations (marijuana, sex, drinking, looseness, idle time, and cursing) have sprung up around me, but I will not fall. I will defeat these things of the world with the grace of You God. I will daily (as I am at this moment) nourish my spirit with Your Word. I will daily let go of myself and let the Holy Spirit within guide me. How can I want sin (things this world presents) when I know the more I give up self, I get double from You God? I can and will continue to do this for Christ sake! For the anointing in me!

As I read Philippians 3:4-11, I pray to not live for the fleshly, physical, outward advantages or should I say disadvantages. Christ has more for me inward!!!!!!

218

As Philippians 3:8 says, "Yes, furthermore, I count everything as loss compared to the possession of the priceless privilege of knowing Christ Jesus my Lord and of progressively becoming more deeply and intimately acquainted with Him. For His sake, I have lost everything and consider it all to be mere rubbish in order that I may win Christ, the anointing."

God, I know my spirit is being changed daily, so that whosoever I meet they will meet Jesus. (It is God's plan in the making so that I may enter Heaven perfect). Thank You for this day God. Thank You.

Put on God's whole armor (the armor of a heavy-armed soldier which God supplies), that you may be able successfully to standup against (all) the strategies and the deceits of the devil. — For we are not wrestling with flesh and blood (contending only with physical opponents), but against the despotisms, against the powers, against (the master spirits who are) the world rulers of this present darkness, against the spirit forces of wickedness in the heavenly (supernatural) sphere. — Therefore put on God' complete armor, that you may be able to resist and stand your ground on the evil day (of danger), and having done all (the crisis demands), to stand (firmly in your place). — Stand therefore (hold your ground), having tightened the belt of truth around your loins and having put on the breastplate of integrity and of moral rectitude and right standing with God, — And having shod your feet in preparation (to face the enemy with the firm-footed stability, the promptness, and the readiness produced by the good news) of the Gospel of peace. — Life up over all the (covering) shield of saving faith, which you can quench all the flaming missiles of the wicked (one). — And take the helmet of salvation and the sword that the spirit wields, which is the word of God. — Pray at all times (on every occasion, in every season) in the Spirit, with all (manner of) prayer and entreaty. To that end keep alert and watch with strong purpose and perseverance, interceding in behalf of all the saints (God's consecrated people).

Ephesians 6:11-18

Keep your guard up! Know that just as God is real; so is satan! He is always in wait to "kill"– "steal"–"destroy." Your choices will keep you in his presence or God's. He knows there is power in "joy" and strives to take it away from you. It is very important that we know how to protect ourselves from the evilness that confronts us daily. We can do that by staying in the Word and, knowing "how and when" to put on the whole (complete) "Armor of God."

<u>August 12, 2002</u>   <u>Monday</u>   <u>7:45 a.m.</u>

Montego Bay, Jamaica

Dear Father God,

I thank You for this day. I thank You for Your love.
I appreciate You!

Well, Father, the weekend has ended, and I still
have a few days ahead of me in Jamaica. I fled sin
for a couple of days, but it seems that no matter how
hard I try or how sincere my heart is in obeying Your
Word, things of this world still partake in my life. I
have fallen into sexual lust, drunkenness, and am
daily tempted with a past habit of smoking marijuana. Forgive me God, in Jesus' name.

I will not give up on myself because I know that will
be giving up on You, and I love You too much to do
that. All I can do is to keep trying and shame the
devil daily. I know that I do not sin today as much
as I did six months ago, and I thank You, Father,
for this change. The "Holy" Spirit that lives within
me has made this change possible. I have continued

to say no to several things of this world, which at one time had control of me. Thank You Jesus. Now, I look forward to conquering even more, with the help of course of the Holy Spirit, and being shown the deceit of satan by the Spirit of Discernment. Stay with me and guide me during the remainder of this challenging, yet defeatable trip. Thank You, in Jesus' name, Amen.

Here's my reading for that day that gave me strength to forgive myself:

O unhappy and pitable and wretched man that I am! Who will release and deliver me from (the shackles of) this body of death? O thank God! (He will!) Through Jesus Christ (the Anointed One) our Lord! So then indeed I of myself with the mind and heart, serve the Law of God, but with the flesh the law of sin. Romans 7:24-25AMP

✻ I fell into some of satan's plan that he had for my trip, but I jumped for joy, as I was able to experience part of God's plan once I repented and asked for change! I was convicted for the sinful acts (sex, marijuana, and looseness) and realized I needed more awareness of God's power within me to say no. The enemy immediately put thoughts into my mind to steal the strength of the Word (with visible things) to make my flesh weak. God still used me, but only when I was not in my flesh. My deepest desire is to be used by God always not just sometimes. I'd rather be used by God than man.

For every wrongdoer hates (loathes, detests) the Light, and will not come out into the Light but shrinks from it, lest his works (his deeds, his activities, his conduct) be exposed and reproved. — But he who practices truth (who does what is right) comes out into the Light; so that his works may be plainly shown to be what they are-wrought with God (divinely prompted, done with God's help, in dependence upon Him).

John 3:20-21 AMP

Do not be conformed to this world (this age), (fashioned after and adapted to its external, superficial customs), but be transformed (changed) by the (entire renewal of your mind (by its new ideals and its new attitude), so that you may prove (for yourselves) what is the good and acceptable and perfect will of God, even the thing which is good and acceptable and perfect (in His sight for you).

Romans 12:2 AMP

✄ Yes, satan really loves to hit you hard; especially when you are experiencing a feeling of guilt. But do not fall into self-condemnation. Always remember our Father is a God of love and forgiveness and mercy. He renews, restores and redeems us through His Son, Jesus Christ. So keep the faith! In Jesus name, Amen!

_____

(Jamaica Trip Continued ...)

Thank You God for using me to bless others during this "sin-filled" trip. It's awesome how You can turn bad into good when we keep our eyes on You. Father, You used me to bless the dinner table of many unsaved adulterers, drunks, foul mouthed, and weed smokers. I was prompted to bless the table, and I did in Jesus' name. Thank You, God. I needed that prayer also as a believer going through the struggles of wanting to please You, but still not completely surrendering to Your ways.

Also, thank You God for making me aware of a wonderful Church service here in Montego Bay. My first day here I had time to myself, because all the guests had not arrived yet. On this first day empty of temptation (people, places, or things) I was guided by the Holy Spirit to a café in the hotel to ask for cereal and for the nearest church of Christ, a Christian Center. Several individuals did not know of such, but God used them to guide me to an older gentleman, by the name of "Rodley" (Bless him). Rodley spoke highly of Jesus Christ and was very aware of some scriptures I was reading that day in the book of Acts. He told me he would secure a ride for me to go to his church in town.

A local Jamaican picked me up by the name of "Rorey" that Sunday. I invited others, but no one wanted to attend. It turned out Rodley (the gentleman who invited me who is also a Deacon at his church) had been trying to get this young man that was my taxi service to church. Well, praise God now he was going because he wanted to make some money for that day. You used me to get him there. Once we arrived, he was going to stay in the car and just wait on me, but something (God) made him come in and stay for the entire service. If I had not listened and let my Holy Spirit guide me neither of us would have been in church. On that day we were both filled with God's Word. The driver "Rorey" was elevated in the Lord, and all he was thinking about at first was making money as driver. He drove me to church that day for God's glory.

The church was "The Church of the Open Bible." The service was preached well by a wonderful Pastor. He spoke on how satan wants us with burdens, how he has a yoke around our necks (a chain), but then he shows in Isaiah 10:27 how God removes these bur-

dens and sets us free from the enemy's choke-hold by the anointing (God's presence). The blood of Jesus has made this possible. Glory to God.

And it shall come to pass in that day, that his burden shall be taken away from off thy shoulder, and his yoke from off thy neck, and the yoke shall be destroyed because of the anointing.

Isaiah 10:27

In Him we have redemption (deliverance and salvation) through His blood, the remission (forgiveness) of our offenses (shortcomings and trespasses), in accordance with the riches and the generosity of His gracious favor.

Ephesians 1:7 AMP

But if we (really) are living and walking in the Light, as He (Himself) is in the Light, we have (true, unbroken) fellowship with one another, and the blood of Jesus Christ His Son cleanses (removes) us from all sin and guilt (keeps us cleansed from sin in all its forms and manifestations).

I John 1:7 AMP

❦ Our Heavenly Father God works in "mysterious ways" which far transcends our understanding. God will use any obedient believer to bring others into His Glory. God is a good God and only wants to see us free; living the good life **now** here on earth! Jesus' obedience on the cross set us free and our obedience here on the earth can set other lost souls free as we are used to bring them to the Lord. Here is where chains will be broken and released from the pain of the past and present bondage experienced here on the earth.

<u>August 13, 2002</u>   <u>Tuesday</u>   <u>7:45 a.m.</u>

Montego Bay, Jamaica

Dear Father God,

Thank You for this day! Thank You for waking me up this morning! Father, all I ask is that You use me for Your will and purpose in this day, please I am all Yours.

Dear precious God, WOW!!! I must note that last night Monday, Aug. 12 around 7 p.m. You spoke to me! I honestly heard Your voice, clear and distinguished for the first time. I was on a smoke-filled bus and my flesh had taken a few puffs of marijuana, even though my spirit had been trying to stay away from it. Thank You for forgiving me, in Jesus' name as I silently asked for help. Although my flesh had done its thing, my spirit was continuously being nourished with Your Word, and received some awesome

words from You! I heard your voice for the first time,
soft and clear with Words of direction and purpose.

My sheep hear my voice, and I know them, and they follow me:
And I give unto them eternal life; and they shall never perish,
neither shall any man pluck them out of my hand.

John 10:27-28

❧ I needed the anointing back to hear from Him. Through my
repentence the anointing or the presence of God came upon me
once again, making it possible for me to hear His voice filled with
the blessing of direction and purpose for my life. So many times
we miss the mark (which is a blessing from God) by staying out
of His presence and indulged in sin.

It was really a unique situation because You shared
with me some of Your perfect will for my life. You told
me what I must do to walk in it. Father You said, I
must leave my three male friends and focus on You
and Your Word. You also told me to write for You. You
told me I would be Your author, for Your glory. You
told me to write on this experience as a testimony.
You said if I give myself completely to You, surrender
and obey, You will take care of me like none other
and all else will fall in place. You said all my hearts
desires would come true. I must first sacrifice myself,
as Jesus did, for Your true peace, and for Your pres-
ence at all times.

You said, while I'm writing for You, You will give me the words. These writings you said will be best sellers from the woman (me) who gave it all up for Jesus' sake so that she may be used to do good works for Your Glory.

You said, I will be married to Jesus until further notice, and I will want for nothing! When the time comes You will bless some man, (it could be one of the three in my life) with my presence, but You will present this man wanting to be saved and used by Jesus or already saved living his life for Jesus, just like me.

God, you know I've received this message so many times in so many different ways, that until I learned to be faithful to Jesus, to You, I would be unable to offer faithfulness and true love to any other aspect of my life (family, work, men, friends, or myself). I guess You knew Father I needed to hear it from You to really take heed to this message.

You said, "I need you to be faithful to Me first!" Wow!! You really do love me more than anybody ever could! Thank You for blessing me with Your Words even in the midst of evil.

❧ The realization of the immense love God has for us can be overwhelming. This love will bring on natural obedience. You must see how much He cares no matter what! God knows exactly what He's getting Himself into when He chooses us. He wants to change us, it hurts His heart to see us trying to change ourselves.

Looking away (from all that will distract) to Jesus, Who is the Leader and the Source of our faith (giving the first incentive for our belief) and is also its Finisher (bringing it to maturity and perfection)...

Hebrews 12:2 AMP

God, You told me to step out and tell my male friends who seem to bring temptation my way that my flesh can't seem to overcome, goodbye (for now)! You also told me to apologize to them for tempting them in any way.

I pray that fear does not enter! It will be a true challenge to tell my male friends goodbye, but I know it's worth it. Jesus is worth it! Anything is worth giving up to have a true personal relationship with You, just like Jesus did while here on the earth!

Give me strength, God, to do as You have spoken and asked me. Please Father, I desire to be obedient in Jesus' name.

This day was a day to remember, my life will truly change from this point on. Thank you for this miracle and awesome testimony of hearing your voice!

Bless (affectionately, gratefully praise) the Lord, you His angels, you mighty ones who do His commandments, hearkening to the voice of His word.   Psalms 103:20 AMP

✌ God turned what the enemy meant for bad to good. He was able to use this moment, when I had fallen, to show me that I was not alone. My steadfast belief, faith, and knowing my rights as a Born-again child of God, saved me; as I repented and called upon the Lord. God knew my heart was sincere. This was a turning point in my Christian walk to move forward boldly. I could finally see the direction and pupose God has for my life. My mind was transformed and all the knowledge I had received thus far was activated! It was like a surge of power plugged into me from the ultimate Source! Now that I have received this power, to keep moving forward I must remain obedient to His words.

✌ Obedience is going to be the key to walk fully in all God has pre-planned for you before you were even formed in your mother's womb. Once again the Holy Spirit has come to help you walk naturally in obedience, just ask Him.

✌ You may ask, "How do I know if I am hearing from God or satan?" As a Born-again believer: God will speak words that **uplift** you and **encourage** you to keep you in His ways; satan will speak words that will **steal** your joy, **kill** your dream, and **destroy** your vision.

Looking away (from all that will distract) to Jesus, Who is the Leader and the Source of our faith (giving the first incentive for our belief) and is also its Finisher (bringing it to maturity and perfection)...

Hebrews 12:2 AMP

Keeping your ears tuned to the Holy Spirit's prompting cannot be emphasized enough! One may not truly realize the valuable, significance of what has just occurred here! (The great revelation knowledge and blessed awareness of anointing; and wisdom of the love of God.)

SPIRIT

But you are not living the life of the flesh you are living the life of the Spirit, if the (Holy) Spirit of God (really) dwells within you (directs and controls you). But if anyone does not possess the (Holy) Spirit of Christ, he is none of His (he does not belong to Christ, is not truly a child of God).

But if Christ lives in you, (then although) your (natural) body is dead by reason of sin and quilt, the spirit is alive because of (the) righteousness (that He imputes to you.

And if the Spirit of Him Who raised up Jesus from the dead dwells in you, (then) He Who raised up Christ Jesus from the dead will restore to life your mortal (short-lived, perishable) bodies through His Spirit who dwells in you.

For if you live according to (the dictates of) the flesh, you will surely die. But if through the power of the (Holy) Spirit your are (habitually) putting to death (making extinct, deadening) the (evil) deeds prompted by the body, you shall (really and genuinely) live forever.

For all who are led by the Spirit of God are sons of God.
Romans 8:9-11, 13-14 AMP

✺ **GOD-PLEASER:** Spirit, soul, and body (in order of importance); God's Wisdom; Maturity in Christ; from a child of God to a son/daughter; addicted to God's Word; handed over my will for God's perfect will; complete satisfaction in my relationship with

Jesus; true peace; true manifestation of all Spiritual gifts seen; prayer in unknown tongue interpretation; true worshipper; in love with Jesus; new heart after consecration (God's heart); obedience comes naturally because of the deep awareness of the Love of God; revelation knowledge (hidden mysteries revealed to the Spirit by the Holy Ghost);in the world, but not of the world; victory over flesh/dead to self; walk in the Spirit; God gets all the glory; Spiritual warfare; **yet more wisdom to receive ...**

(Reference: Apostles Prophets, by Dr. Bill Hamon)

<u>August 21, 2002</u>   <u>Wednesday</u>   <u>10:20 p.m.</u>

Dear Father God,

Thank You for such a blessed day filled with the opportunity to serve others! Thank You!

God, I realize I have not written in my journal for seven days. Wow, there's the number seven again! (Seven reflects completion). It took me seven days to receive and act on Your message of obedience in Jamaica. Seven days for me to receive strength through prayer to make it manifest. I love You and know You keep me protected daily.

You specifically told me to step away from my male friends and apologize to them for bringing temptation their way. You told me to learn how to be faithful to Jesus and all else would fall into place. Well ...

Just yesterday over the telephone I told my most recent male friend Kenny that I was sorry. Kenny is a great guy, very unique and awesome, but it seems like Kenny knows God because he grew up in the church, but he doesn't display a personal relationship with Jesus because he is not conscious of his sins. It doesn't seem to bother him. So, I apologized for all the temptation and un-Godly things that were part of our friendship before he was traded to play baseball in another city. Those un-Godly things included: gossip, sex, debating; things carnal Christians do. He heard me and accepted my apology, but was giggling a little because he could not understand why I was doing this. All I could say to him was, "One day you will understand why I had to ask for Your forgiveness for doing wrong to You and with You, for my peace of mind. God is a God of justice and there will be penalties for those who wrong other people. He is a forgiving God, but also a God of justice."

I also had to tell Kenny I didn't care if he thought it was weird, because daily I'm being prepared to be a God-pleaser, not a man-pleaser! I'll probably never hear from him again, not unless you (God) renew his mind. This would be His choice, of course.

Oh well, I can give up all for Jesus' sake, with the help of the Holy Spirit. One down, two to go ...

I also apologized to KG, who is, seeking God in his

own way, but doesn't know Jesus personally. I asked him to forgive me for the past years of sins we were involved in. Just a few months ago my flesh (sex) had been stronger than my will concerning him. I asked for forgiveness and continue to pray and wait on the day to just stand and say no!

This among other things has always been a strong part of my and KG's relationship. I know we love each other and have a lot in common, but Jesus is not one of them. Oh well. He didn't take me too serious. He told some children who were asking him for an autograph that day to call me his wife (of course this would be in his timing, it would be after he has renewed mind, without Jesus). That very same afternoon he hinted a little afternoon "dessert." I said, "No, I hope you accept my apology once again," and I left.

KG still calls, but I know he is starting to listen. I must continue to stand firm on keeping Christ first. One day KG will really take my new walk seriously. I know it will be when my stand stays firm! God is working on him. Two down!

And there's still Mark to go ...

If you will listen diligently to the voice of the Lord your God, being watchful to do all His commandments which I command you this day, the Lord your God will set you high above all nations of the earth. And all these blessings shall come upon you and overtake you if you heed the voice of the Lord your God.

Deuteronomy 28:1-2 AMP

❧ The more you crucify the flesh (carnal, lower-self), the weaker it becomes and will eventually (shall I dare say?) become satisfied; surrendering control to your (spirit-filled, upper-self). Obedience, prayer, and persistence play an important role in your spiritual growth.

<u>August 30, 2002</u>   <u>Friday</u>   <u>1:48 p.m.</u>

Dear Heavenly Father,

Thank You for your Spirit, thank you for redemption from the curses of this world. Thank You for setting me free!

God I don't know exactly what is going on in me, but I know You are using me for something incredible! I'm watching Benny Hinn's healing service on television (TBN) and the Spirit had me speaking in tongues over and over! I don't know who or what I was praying for, but You used me at that moment. As I prayed I felt Your hands embrace me like never before. They were huge and comforting. I know why I feel so safe.

Use me more!! Please!!! I feel great knowing that You can do great work through me.

Thank You for taking care of me, God. I love You and appreciate You.

(For it is He) Who rescued and saved us from such a perilous death, and He will still rescue and save us; in and on Him we have set our hope (our joyful and confident expectation) that He will again deliver us (from danger and destruction and draw us to Himself).

Corinthians 1:10 AMP

❧ Seeking God first, increases the awareness of His daily presence in your life as well as His divine purpose for your existence. He touches your heart with His love, comforting you. Continue to fellowship with your Heavenly Father; talking with Him in prayer. There's no better listener than He.

September 3, 2002   Tuesday   4:30 p.m.

Dear Father God,

People continue to say I talk too much or they say I ramble. Dear Father use my mouth to ramble for You! For Your glory! Thank You.

God, thank You for letting me have such a wonderful day with my two best friends, Sharon and Tasha yesterday. We had the best time. It was filled with love, laughter, joy and peace. We know it all came from You. We had the opportunity to lift up Your name, and speak of how Your precious Son, Jesus Christ is working in our lives. Sharon and myself are on the same page and have a true desire to get to know You daily. We do this by reading Your Word, studying Your Word, and living Your Word therefore experiencing the reality of Your Word.

Now Tasha seems to have different (characteristics) I honestly do not know if she truly believes that You love her just the same as us all. I know the only way she'll find out is by hearing Your Word and by reading Your Word more and more.

I've realized someone can be "Born Again" and let Jesus come live in-and-through You, but he or she also needs to feed this new Spirit with Your Word Father, the Bible, for true manifestation of the power inside. Most of all we have to believe this!

Bible = Basic Instructions Before Leaving Earth (My girlfriend Sharon told me this a good while ago).

So, I pray dear heavenly Father that Tasha becomes aware of a more intimate relationship with Jesus. That she falls in love with Him like never before! Jesus can heal us everywhere we hurt!! I didn't know I was so empty even with all that I had in front of me!!!

For let him that wants to enjoy life and see good days...Let him turn away from wickedness and shun it, and let him do right. Let him search for peace and seek it eagerly. (Do not merely desire peaceful relations with God, ... but pursue, go after them!) I Peter 3:10-11 AMP

🌿 Once you have fallen in love with the reality of Jesus it will be shown in the way you live. You will no longer desire the things of the world. You will want to meditate on the word of God day and night. His way will turn into a natural way of living, not your old ways. The desire to get to know Him more personal will be evident. Not only at sunday service or mid-week Bible study.

September 3, 2002   Tuesday   4:56 p.m.

Dear Heavenly Father,

Forgive me (as I know that You already have) for not knowing over the past 32 years the true importance of Your Son, Jesus Christ.

So many people go through life ignorant of the sacrifice Jesus made for us. But at the tender age of 33, I now know and have a true love for both of You. I know that it was predestined for me to be free at this moment, by reading this in the Bible,

And we know that all things work together for good to them that love God, to them who are called according to his purpose...For whom He did foreknow (knew beforehand), he also did predestinate to be conformed to the image of His Son, that He might be the firstborn among many brethen.
Romans 8:28-29 AMP

Over the past five years or so I attended church, and prayed to You, but never really acknowledging Jesus Christ as I do now. Thank You. I now know that the only way to have a personal relationship with You is through Your Son, Jesus. For it says in the Bible, "If you deny me on earth, I will deny you before my father in Heaven." (Matthew 10:33)

Who is (such a) liar as he who denies that Jesus is the Christ (the Messiah)? He is the antichrist (the antagonist of Christ), who (habitually) denies and refuses to acknowledge the Father and the Son." "No one who (habitually) denies (disowns) the Son ever has the Father. Whoever confesses (acknowledges and has) the Son has the Father also.

I John 2:22-23 AMP

I used to think (before being "Born Again") that my pastor was giving me the power through her word, and when he or she would reference the Bible I would never go prove to myself what they were preaching. It wasn't until "I" started reading the scriptures that were directed my way, did I start truly believing I am the great expression of God, as His son Jesus is. I am joint-heirs with Jesus and I deserve all that God promised. We are one. I am married to Jesus! Hallelujah!!!

Now to me the Bible is not like reading another language it's an addiction. It's an good addiction. When I read it I feel like the words jump out and into my

Spirit. The Bible is actually filled with energy. It brightens my day, answers my questions, and guides me in the right direction, always! It's one of my best friends.

I love You, God!!!

Blessed and fortunate and happy and spiritually prosperous (in that state in which the born-again child of God enjoys His favor and salvation) are those who hunger and thirst for righteousness (uprightness and right standing with God), for they shall be completely satisfied!

Matthew 5:6 AMP

❧ The best high in the world is reading the word of God and letting the reality of the Bible fill your every void as it defines who you really are; the great expression of your Heavenly Father! If you are hungry for His presence in your life you will finally be completely satisfied.

September 8, 2002   Sunday   8:45 a.m.

Thank You for giving me the gift of this day! Thank You for the new Tracy L. Moss! Thank You for a marriage to Your son, Jesus Christ, so that He may, through me, do good works for Your glory!!!

Dear Father God I thank You for letting the Holy Spirit (Your nature) change things in me that I felt I could not change by myself. I have been redeemed from sex!!! Hallelujah! No more will I desire it, until I'm making love to my husband. All penalties for this sin that continued to conquer me after being "Born Again" are over now!! Once and for all! I now look forward daily to the great rewards that are Your promise when Your children give up something (big or small sins are all the same) for Your will and not the will of the enemy. God, You give us double for our trouble with great rewards.

But without faith it is impossible to please and be satisfactory to Him. For whoever would come near to God must (necessarily) believe that God exists and that He is the rewarder of those who diligently seek Him (out).

Hebrews 11:6 AMP

Now God here is another challenge I pray for the Holy Spirit (Your nature) to help me conquer: Yes, "Born Again" and I still have challenges daily ...

My career as a Mercedes-Benz salesperson is a true blessing. I am able to serve Your people and others

245

(non-believers). God, You are blessing me financially daily through this gift from You, but I feel like I am the only "light" in a dark place. Lately, I find I'm telling lies to customers under the counsel of my management team. Sometimes I don't realize it or intentionally do it, but I notice it as soon as it comes out of my mouth. This isn't right! I'm not a man (the world) pleaser, I am a God pleaser and this has to change Holy Spirit! I pray God that as I take my stand to be honest and true only, even if it means losing a customer or approval of management, that You will keep me safe from any harm.

I pray that management be removed before me, if it comes to that, as I stand in integrity. I can't tell a lie, it is not my new nature. I am convicted each time I attempt to. Thank You God for answered prayer in Jesus' name, Amen.

But no weapon that is formed against you shall prosper, and every tongue that shall rise against you in judgment you shall show to be in the wrong. This (peace, righteousness, security, triumph over opposition) is the heritage of the servants of the Lord.

Isaiah 54:17a AMP

God I also wanted to thank You for using me to minister to people, to uplift and edify them with Your Word and Your truth. Sometimes I don't remember what You said through me when I minister, but I know how powerful the words are just by the captive look in the eyes of those listening. This has happened many times, and I didn't write it down, but I will start doing my best with it. Just yesterday I was going to a beach bash where my friend Denise's boyfriend's band was playing. I was walking from my car and heard three older gentlemen speaking on how the commandments where destroyed. I did not say anything at that time, but the Holy Spirit in me had me go back.

I remember one of the older gentlemen saying, "God does not have a son," and that's when You began to use me. I preached about Jesus and how You can't have a relationship with God without acknowledging His Son. I spoke of the traumatic change in me once the Holy Spirit arrived. One gentleman told me, "You are a great speaker."
(I received this as You saying, You were proud of me for sharing Your Word. I know You can speak through anyone).

They had so many debates that I didn't visit; I just spoke on the goodness of Jesus and how much He loves us. I spoke on how this incredible peace has overflowed my body, and how believing Jesus is Lord has changed my old way of thinking and living. I just know it's better than ever!

They asked, "What is your religion?" I said I do not follow a "religious" way of serving the Lord, for it is not of my works that I am saved. I am a Christian in the body of Christ; I let Him guide me however He pleases by the Holy Spirit within me. I told them when Heaven arrives the only thing God will want to know is, "Did you accept my Son as your Lord and Savoir?" Not if are you Baptist, Jewish, Catholic or otherwise.

Also as the Holy Spirit led me, I responded to them concerning why there are so many wars. I told them God gives us choices and our choices lead to consequences.

Who are they to question God? God said in the book of Genesis, "Let there be light, and there was light!" We'd better stop questioning the Creator!

🌿 Keep your Faith in God. Tackle problems as they come. Know that God will hear your prayers. Keep order in your life (don't be double-minded). Have no fear of man for greater is He that is within you than he (satan) that is in the world. Share your experiences of salvation by testifying of God's goodness and works in your life. When the Holy Spirit calls, follow.

September 12, 2002   Thursday   11:15 p.m.

Thank You dear Father for this day filled with Your promises: peace, security, ministry, understanding, love, joy, and an awesome hunger for Your Word!

But without faith it is impossible to please and be satisfactory to Him. For whoever would come near to God must (necessarily) believe that God exists and that He is the rewarder of those who earnestly and diligently seek Him (out).

Hebrews 11:6 AMP

🌿 That's just a few of His many promises. Here's a few more: faithfulness, strength, wisdom, prosperity, comfort, integrity, love, love, love, and true love.

September 13, 2002   Friday   7:15 a.m.

Thank You for the "Faith Conference" I've been attending all week at my new church home, Living Word Christian Center! I am being made aware of faith to do the impossible! Bless all the pastors You have sent to share Your Word. I will be giving a personal summary in my journal once it ends today or tomorrow. I must share all the good news I'm receiving.

Your Word God is like a drug (a good drug) that keeps me wanting more and more. My spirit hungers for it. There is truly action and life in the Word!!

Study to show thyself approved unto God, a workman that needeth not to be asjamed, rightly dividing the word of truth.

II Timothy 2:15

My people are destroyed for lack of knowledge: becuse thou hast rejected knowledge.

Hosea 4:6a

🌿 Do not be afraid to venture! God is everywhere! Just as Jesus was curious and wanted to learn what He could, so should we seek the knowledge and wisdom and experiences of Christ. The Holy Spirit leads, we follow; in faith.

September 16, 2002   Monday   6:20 a.m.

Good morning Father God,

Thank You for letting me wake up this morning, thank You!

Well almost a month ago you spoke to me in Jamaica and told me what to do when it came to my male relationships. (This is finally the completion of the Aug. 21 entry.)

I found it very challenging to say goodbye to Mark. He was the most "real brother" I'd ever met. He accepted me for me, and I tried to accept him for him, until my change, my "Born Again" walk ...You see, Mark knows God, at least he thinks he does. He thinks he has a personal relationship with God. With all that said, he hates to hear me say God's name, and he doesn't acknowledge God's Son at all. He obviously does not know that it is through God's Son only, that we have a personal relationship with our Father.

Now, I really do love Mark and could see him as my [mate] for life, but I can't and will not do that without him being "Born Again." He has to accept Jesus Christ as his Lord and repent for all his past and present sins by letting Jesus (God's nature) come inside him. He must want this change.

"You lose yourself when you become religious," he says. He also says that God can only do so much, you have to guide yourself.

God, I know that You will make him aware in order to accept Jesus in his heart, (the Holy Spirit); he will have to die to self. I am dying daily to selfish ways, and to things that please my flesh, and pray God that You do the same in him. This new refreshed person will recognize the Spirit man that has been planted as a seed. This new seed has to be nurtured daily with the Word of our Father God, the Bible. Mark would not listen to me much on how he could remove his burdens of stress, anger, loneliness, and many other characteristics of his lost soul. These are characteristics of satan that continue to keep us in bondage to him.

I desire Father, if I am to have a companion in my

life that he hunger for God's Word as I do. That he not "cut me off" when I mention Your goodness. At times, with Mark it was as if he wanted to get this "God" awareness that I had first, and that he was envious of the relationship I was building with Jesus. I do believe You have tried to get to him in the past, but it's all about us choosing You, as I finally have.

So, I continued to get revelations, and messages on how I must give up something "precious" to me that I may see the results I desire. My precious seed was Mark.

He has been a precious seed planted for Jesus sake! My harvest will be a new "Born Again" Mark who hungers for You, God, and has or wants to have Jesus as Lord. If this is not Your will, God You will bless me with another. I believe this and receive it! I will not question the goodness of You God in this decision.

I am obedient to Your Words set forth to me in Jamaica. God I look forward to my harvest.

Sometimes You have to give up what is precious to receive more of Your blessings. Thank You God, in Jesus' name for this revelation.

🌿 God sacrificed his Son Jesus Christ for our redemption. Is it too much to ask, that we sacrifice our worldly desires for Christ's sake? (The good life, His father wants us to live, for an eternity.)

It seems that some Christians think they have to suffer to get good results from people or things, but I believe it is a choice. I had to give up on someone else, before I gave up on myself. God is in control and He only wants good for me now and to come!

Here is the letter I wrote to Mark after having a conversation in the middle of the night that did not go so well. He was hurt and could not understand why I was ending our friendship for now.

September 17, 2002
Tuesday 10 a.m.

Hello Mr. Allen,

I have enclosed in this envelope a tape that has been with me since my born-again walk, back in March. This is one of the many teachings that have bought me closer to knowing who we truly are as children of God and as brothers and sisters to Jesus Christ. I can't seem to explain to you verbally what is happening to me, so maybe if you can find it in your heart to read this letter, and listen to this tape you will understand more clearly.

Mark, what I realized is that when I continued to hear of so many different ways to view God (religions) I was confused. It wasn't until I started seeking and reading the Bible myself that God brought me the realization that the only way I could have a personal relationship with Him was to acknowledge His Son, Jesus, and let Him come live in my heart and forgive me for my past sins. From that day forward I let Him guide me daily to the plan He has for my life, for His Glory.

Jesus said to him, "I am the way, and the truth, and the life; no one comes to the Father, but through Me." John 14:6

You see, from studying God's Word, He helps us to understand some of His ways of doing things and why. But when we listen to other people without proving it our selves, we can be misled and misguided, thus continuing to live in the world's turmoil _without_ His hand on us.

Baby, I used to think that if I completely surrendered my life to God that I wouldn't have any more fun and I'd have to change everything. That's far from the truth. Now of course, I do not desire to do some of the things I used to, but I'm truly enjoying life more abundantly! Free from worry, free from punishing myself for past and present mistakes, free from confusion, free from guilt, free from jealousy, free from anger, free from being a liar, free from depression, free from being anxious, free from lack, free from making the wrong decisions, free from fear and free from the "choke hold" satan had had on my life for 32 years.

Now, I make mistakes, and I know God will forgive me as soon as I ask him to. I do not worry because I know all is for good no matter how it looks. I do not get confused because I seek God's counsel before I do anything. I now know how to truly love. I am now patient; I am now at peace, so I do not let anger overcome me. I now recognize prosperity in my life along with growth in my finances. I can no longer lie. I forgive and forget any wrong done to me because I know my Father will bring justice to the situation, I fear nothing! This is not an overnight process; God changes us in His time. Five years from now, we will not sin as much as we do now; it's His promise. We just have to recognize that it's through his Son, Jesus that this change is occurring and not of ourselves. We can all experience this.

For by grace are ye saved through faith; and not that of yourselves; it is a gift of God: Lest any man (male or female) should boast or brag. Ephesians 2:8-9

Each day I am excited to wake up and see how God is going to use me to assist in carrying out His good plan for all our lives.

He loves us all the same and wants us all to be released from what the world has to offer, found in John 10:10: "The enemy (the world, satan) comes to steal, kill, and destroy, but I come that you may have life and have it more abundantly!"

I do love you Mark, with all my heart and I promise I have not given up on you, but God is in control right now and I trust that He will mend whatever it takes for us to prosper together, if it's His Will. Baby, we can't even begin to imagine the great things He is working on right now in our lives. Explanations are not visible at this moment, we just have to be patient and wait for the great results of His plan.

God Bless You, Handsome,
Tracy

Commit your way to the Lord (roll and repose each care of your load on Him); trust (lean on, rely on, and be confident) also in Him and He will bring it to pass. 6 And He will make your uprightness and right standing with God go forth as the light, and your justice and right as (the shining sun of) the noonday.

Psalms 37:5 AMP

❧ No greater love is there in man, than the love of Jesus, who died to save us all. God must come first in our lives! Without God in our lives, we are nothing! He is the creator and the maker of all things.

September 18, 2002   Wednesday   10:30 p.m.

I love You God! There's something about the name Jesus! There's something about the name Jesus!

The power of this name has given me the revelation that whenever old behavior or thoughts surface in my mind to just say JESUS, over and over. All my wrong thoughts become erased at that moment. I am at peace instantly!

Thank You God for Your Son!

I love you both!!! With the knowing that You are one!

Jesus approached and, breaking the silence, said to them, All authority (all power of rule) in heaven and on earth has been given to Me.

Matthew 28:18 AMP

❧ There is power and peace in the name of "JESUS."

BRING THEM TO ME

My Final Letter to the Lord in Preparation for Journal #2:

Thank you for walking with me in Journal #1 and sharing in my deep thoughts and intimate letters to the Lord. As I wrote, the Lord was teaching me and my hope is you have also received some of His wisdom by reading along. Make a choice as I did to come to know God through Christ Jesus so that you may walk in the fullness of a life already prepared for you since the beginning.

Remember anything that distracts you from getting to know the Living God is a "road block." You can't move forward until you ask for the Lord's assistance. Cry out and stop wasting precious time living a life God has not intended for you to live. Our loving Father places examples directly in front of us so that we can be saved from self and death when trying to please the world. You must know there is real hope for a brighter future no matter what your past or present is. This hope is Jesus. I am your peer example as He is our Ultimate example. We have to know Him in order to truly know what path to follow.

My intimate walk with the Lord continues in the second part of "Bring Them To Me." You will share and learn with me as I go the extra mile to do whatever it takes to get to know God through my personal relationship with Jesus. My hunger and desire is to stay in His presence so that I can distinguish between whom "exactly" I am hearing from (God or satan), and to be led by the Leader of my destiny as it has been ordained. My Spirit will come first, then my soul, and my body because it is by my Spirit that I am able to understand the unseen.

I will be in this world, but not of this world by simply choosing to get to know the Lord's way of thinking and living as I read His Word, the Living Bible. My Spirit will also guide me towards more life changing scriptures. These scriptures will guide both my own and your future steps as we continue on a deeper walk filled with miracles and wonders.

No more keeping God "in a box" until Sundays roll around. I want all that My Father has for me, and so should you. I will worship, praise, and adore Him as I get to know Him on a more personal level. My entries continue to reflect how He is my everything and the results of this acceptance in my life. I not only speak about how much I love Him, you will read exactly how my life has changed because I now live for Him and not the world. Continue to walk with me as I take you further into His presence as I strive to the next Spiritual level; knowing how to say "no" to my flesh and "yes" to my Spirit.

I have prepared a prayer and confession to the Lord in preparation for the second part of the "Bring Them To Me" series. This will assist you and me in standing on the promises of God for those who believe. This prayer will bring you courage and boldness to walk into the next spiritual level God is calling you to.

Our ultimate goal is to walk more in the spirit and less in the flesh.

Covenant to Stay in His Presence

1. I come to you in agreement Lord because you have set before me life and death, blessings and curses, and I chose life. *I have said "yes" to your perfect will, and no to mine. In accordance to your will, I have been made holy, (free from sin) through the offering made <u>once and for all</u> of the body of Jesus Christ. *Therefore I will invite conviction and I will not condemn myself.

2. In the Bible you define me, refine me, and show me a new way. The world showed me a way that seemed right for many years but the end result is death. *Thank you for saving me by your Grace. Your promises are true to me because I am now filled with your nature and you delight in the prosperity of my soul. *

3. My ways and my doings have brought (past) things upon me. I have confessed and admitted my sins and have been cleansed and forgiven from all that is ungodly. *I did not know and understand you. I was a thickheaded child with no "real" understanding. *But now you have spoken, and I have a purpose, I will not relent or turn back from getting to know you. *

4. Before you formed me in my mother's womb you knew and approved of me as your chosen instrument, and before I was born you separated me and set me apart and appointed me to be a great

woman of the nations. *With this knowing I will seek, aim at and strive first after your kingdom and your righteousness and all other things will be added to me. *

5. Lord now that I am your born again child, and I know not how to begin or to finish in this new way of living; so I ask one thing of you; that you might give me an understanding mind (wisdom) and a hearing heart that I may discern between good and bad. I know that this request has pleased you, because I have not asked for long life or for riches, or for the life of my enemies but I have asked for myself understanding to recognize what is just and right. I know You have done as I asked. Thank you. You have given me a wise discerning mind and you have given me wisdom. You have also because of my unselfish prayer given me those things I did not ask for, both riches and honor so that I will not be equal to this world. *

6. I will love you, Lord because you first loved me, and I will obey your voice and cling to you. You are my life and the length of my days. *My diligence to observe and to do all you command will set me high above. Blessings will continue to come on me and overtake me. I will be blessed coming in, and blessed going out. You will cause my enemies who rise against me to be defeated before my face, and you will establish me as Holy unto you. *For it is written in your word Lord, that eye has not seen and ear has not heard and has not entered into the heart of man all that God has prepared for those who

love Him. * I am prepared by the Holy Spirit for all that you have for me to do Lord Jesus.

7. I will strip myself of my former nature, discarding my old un-renewed self with its worldly lust, and be constantly renewed in the spirit of my mind, having a fresh mental and spiritual attitude. My meditation day and night will be on your word. * I will put on a new nature created in God's image. * I will therefore be an imitator of God, copying and following his example shown in you my Lord. I am just like you Jesus. We are well-loved children imitating our Heavenly Father. *

8. Because I put all my trust in you Lord and have made this walk my final resting place, you have given your angels special charge over me to accompany me and defend and preserve me in all my ways of obedience and service to you. I will call on you and you will answer me and deliver me honoring me with long life and showing me your salvation. * My thirsty soul follows hard after you and your right hand holds me up. *

9. Holding on to this testimony of the truth of God, I will constant-ly strip and throw aside every unnecessary weight and sin that clings to and entangles me keeping me heavy with burden. I will run with patience, and endurance actively showing persistence in this appoint-ed course of the Christian race that you have set before me. I will

look away from all that will distract me from you Lord Jesus because you are my leader and the source of my faith. You are my finisher bringing me to maturity and perfection. *

10. Yes, Lord it is my goal to count everything as a loss compared to the possession of the priceless privilege of knowing you and of progressively becoming more deeply and intimately acquainted with you. I look forward to perceiving, recognizing, and understanding you more strongly and more clearly. I must remain in your presence, which lifts me out from among the dead, even while in this body. I will forget the past and reach toward those things that are ahead, pressing toward the mark for the prize of your high calling made available to me because I believe in the Christ, the anointing that is within me. *

11. Lord you have placed the Holy Spirit in me and I will call on Him always for help to change those things I can't seem to change, that I may stay in your presence. *The Holy Spirit is my helper, teacher, counselor, comforter, and intercessor waiting in expectation to complete His assignment in bringing me from gory to glory. I will ask for help everyday. When I can't seem to find the right words to pray, He will pray for me in an unknown tongue. * I will pray with perseverance. *

12. No thing will be impossible for me to do because it is not I, but

it is the power that I received when the Holy Spirit came upon me. * With the acknowledgement of the Christ in me I will always be led in triumph and through me Lord you will spread and make evident the sweet smelling fragrance of the knowledge of our Father God everywhere with boldness. *

13. I will no longer have emptiness in my life because I have descend and am now the same as you Lord who has ascend high above all the Heavens making Your presence fill all things. * We share the same mind, the mind of Christ. * Your presence fills me with wisdom, knowledge, faith, healing, miracles, discernment and the praying of tongues. * And so Lord I know that all these powerful spiritual gifts that live in me are necessary but, they are all useless and with no effect if I do not have Love. * I walk in peace knowing that you have replaced my heart with your heart because I asked. I am now filled with Love, because our Father God is Love.

14. On this day I have put you into remembrance of your word as it is written. * Therefore I am assured and know that all will work together for my good because I love God and am called according to His purpose. * In Jesus' name, Amen.

Paragraph	Scriptures in order of appearance with *
1	(Deut. 30:19) (Hebrews 10:10)
2	(Proverbs 16:25) (3 John 2)
3	(I John 1:9) (Jeremiah 4:18-21) (Jeremiah 4:28)
4	(Jeremiah 1:5) (Matthew 6:33)
5	(I Kings 3:9-13)
6	(Deut. 30:20) (Deut. 28:1-14) (I Cor. 2:9)
7	(Joshua 1:8) (Eph. 4:22) (Eph. 5:1)
8	(Psalms 91) (Psalms 63:1 & 8)
9	(Hebrews 12:1-2)
10	(Philippians 3:8-14)
11	(Romans 7:25) (Acts 2:4) (I Thes. 5:17)
12	(Acts 1:8) (2 Cor. 2:14)
13	(Eph. 4:10) (I Cor. 2:16) (I Cor. 12:8-11) (I Cor. 13:13)
14	(Isaiah 43:26) (Romans 8:28)

"Bring Them To Me" Journal #2 will be coming soon.
Walk more in the Spirit with me.

For more information about our author or
to order this book please contact:

In Time Publishing & Media Group
75 East Wacker Drive, 10th Floor
Chicago, Illinois 60601
Tel: (312) 419-9100
Fax: (312) 419-9400
www.intimepublishing.com
www.360degreeministry.com